The First Baptist Church of Charlotte

FRANCES FIELDEN EPPLEY

The
First Baptist Church
of Charlotte

Its Heritage

CHARLOTTE, NORTH CAROLINA
1981

PRINTED IN THE UNITED STATES OF AMERICA
HERITAGE PRINTERS, INC.
CHARLOTTE, NORTH CAROLINA

Contents

Illustrations follow page 42.

Acknowledgments

Many friends and members of the church provided information, materials, and photographs toward the making of this book. Among them are Ree Sheets, Frances Howell, Mr. and Mrs. B. H. Fitzgerald, Mr. and Mrs. J. Russell Smith, Claudia Odom Mitchell, M. G. Perry, Ruby Caudle, Joe Burnette, Eugene Warren, Sara Anne Smith, Myrtle Haywood, Marie Nolan, Mr. and Mrs. C. C. Hope, Jr., Joan Hope, Rae Padgett, Buford Cromer, Betty Haithcock, Libby and Ed Wells, members of the Three-B Baraca Class, Dixie Martin, and church librarian Agnes Gilliam.

Special thanks go to Marie Roberts for answering numerous questions from her extensive knowledge of the church, and to Paul Wyche for his research and drawings of the first two meeting houses. Gratitude is due Harvey Brown, Sr., Mrs. G. M. Hampton, and Mr. and Mrs. Paul Gilliam for their work in compiling the appendix. Much appreciation is felt for those who expressed interest and encouragement during the more than three years of research and writing.

Gratitude is given to Ann Burnette and Mary Hazel Hatchette for copy-reading the manuscript, and to Mary Ann Lewis for typing it. Appreciation is given to G. M. Hampton, Charles Haithcock, and others of the church finance committee who arranged the publishing of the book. The author and the church are greatly indebted to Mae and C. C Hope, Jr., for their competent promotion of its sale.

Chapter 1 | Its Heritage Before 1832

There were two routes by which the Baptists first came to the South. One was by way of the sea from New England to the coast of South Carolina some miles north of Charleston. The other was by way of the Great Wagon Road from Pennsylvania through Virginia into North Carolina and into South Carolina. In an extraordinary way the two paths merged in the events which led to the birth of the First Baptist Church of Charlotte. Today the members of the still vibrant, thriving church are the possessors of a remarkable heritage.

The roots of this heritage lie in the convictions and the courage of Baptist believers in the American colonies during the seventeenth and eighteenth centuries. Among the Baptists in New England persecuted in varying degrees by the officials of the Massachusetts Bay Colony was a convert named William Screven. Screven, who had come from England and had become a successful merchant, was licensed to preach after his conversion by the leaders of the Baptist church in Boston. Through his efforts, there was established a small Baptist church in Kittery, Maine, a village of independent sea-faring people.

Following the purchase of Maine by the Massachusetts Bay Colony, William Screven was imprisoned because of his religious beliefs, then released and ordered to leave the colony. With the entire congregation of the Kittery church, seventeen souls in all, he sailed from the rock-bound Kittery coast and came to the shores of South Carolina. In this southern colony where there was religious tolerance as well as some old acquaintances from England, Screven bought 1500 acres of land 40 miles north of Charleston and called the area Somerton.

1

At the same time, scattered along the coast of South Carolina were other individuals and groups who were Anabaptists, General Baptists, Particular Baptists, Separate Baptists, and Regular Baptists. These were people who did not agree about the details of grace and free will, but who were — in fundamental doctrines — Baptists and who believed in and exercised the freedom to differ. Called by different names and not yet organized into any congregation as far as is known, these believers like countless groups before them had in common two characteristics of faith. First, they reserved baptism for those who were old enough to make a personal profession of faith and commitment to Jesus Christ as Lord and Savior. Second, they believed in the independent and individual interpretation of the Holy Scriptures. Their faith was distinctively compatible with the growing urge for independence among many of the American colonists. For they believed in the complete separation of church and state and held civil and religious liberty to be an inalienable right of all people.

When Screven again moved his flock from Somerton to Charleston, a number of the coastal Baptists were gathered into his congregation. Under Screven's leadership, they were welded into one Baptist body and later were given a lot on Church Street for a meeting house. They were constituted into the First Baptist Church of Charleston on July 18, 1699. This church, which dates its beginning to the group in Somerton and is still active, has the honor and prestige of being the oldest Baptist church in the South.

The Charleston church grew and prospered and had among its early able and dedicated leaders a pastor named Richard Furman, a brilliant and self-educated minister whose Baptist family had come to the South from New York State. While pastor of the Charleston church, Furman was one of the 33 delegates from 11 states who gathered in May of 1814 in Philadelphia to form the General Missionary Convention of the Baptist Denomination of the United States of America for Foreign Missions. This body was the first Baptist foreign missionary society and represented the first centralization of the Baptists in the United States. Richard Furman was offered the first presidency of the convention, but because of the distances involved he declined. His ideas concerning the work and organization of this convention were later used by the men who formed the Southern Baptist Convention.

Furman believed strongly in providing an education for young preachers, and largely through his efforts and influence the Furman Theological Institution was established. This school, which bore his name, was the forerunner of Furman University and the parent school of the Southern Baptist Theological Seminary. The seminary was first a part of the Furman Institution located in Greenville, South Carolina, and later was moved to Louisville, Kentucky.

Richard Furman, a great patriot of the new nation which had been formed by the American Revolution and a churchman whose influence extended far beyond his own lifetime, had seventeen children. Among them was James Furman, the preacher boy from the Furman Theological Institution who was invited with a companion named Mr. Barnes, also a young preacher, to come to Charlotte in the summer of 1832 to hold a revival meeting. From this meeting there emerged the initial organization of the First Baptist Church of Charlotte.

The other route by which Baptists came to the South was along the Great Wagon Road, which began in Philadelphia and extended as far south as Savannah, Georgia. Originally it was a network of Indian trails called The Great Warriors' Path, stretching along the ridges east of the Appalachian Mountains. As the trails of the red man gave way to the wagons and stagecoaches of the white settlers, great numbers of colonists moved along this path toward the southern and western frontiers, seeking more plentiful and cheaper land for their homesteads.

The settlers were English, Swiss, Scotch-Irish, Welsh, and German. As to religion they were Presbyterians, Methodists, True Lights, Quakers, Moravians, and Baptists. Among the Baptist churches established along the Wagon Road were some of the historic churches of North Carolina, including the Reedy Creek Church (or Fishing Creek Church) in 1750 in Warren County and the Sandy Creek Church in 1755 in what is now Chatham County. During the same period the Scotch-Irish migrated from Pennsylvania to Mecklenburg to dot the county with their seven original

Presbyterian churches: Sugar Creek, Steele Creek, Hopewell, Poplar Tent, Center, Providence, and Philadelphia.

Charlotte was among the towns which marked the Great Wagon Trail as it stretched southward, others being Roanoke, Rocky Mount, Salem, Salisbury, Rock Hill, Chester, and Augusta. While Charlotte was one of the villages which provided inns or taverns with lodging and food for wayfarers, and although many settlers came to the area, only a sprinkling of Baptists arrived in Mecklenburg. Concerning the scarcity of Baptists in the county, Dr. T. J. Taylor in an article, "Early Baptist Efforts In Charlotte," published in the *North Carolina Baptist Historical Papers* in 1899, wrote, "There is no account of any Baptist residing in the neighborhood of Charlotte until toward the close of the eighteenth century. The absence of record does not necessarily prove that there were no Baptists among the early settlers; for in the midst of a strongly Presbyterian population, and with no church organization, a few isolated Baptists would have had no opportunity of putting themselves on record as such."

However, across the county's southern border there was established in 1792 a Baptist church called Sugar Creek or Flint Hill, whose members and pastor had arrived by way of The Great Wagon Road. This church, still active, was located between Fort Mill and Sugar Creek, twelve miles south of Charlotte. If the First Baptist Church of Charlotte had a mother church, it was the Flint Hill Baptist Church.

The story of the Flint Hill Church is obtained largely from the records of that church, from the article by Dr. Taylor, and from the writings of Dr. T. J. Pritchard, who was the pastor of the First Baptist Church of Charlotte from 1893 to 1896. A lovely old church built in 1907 stands today on the original Flint Hill site atop a wooded knoll, with a beautifully landscaped and weathered cemetery nearby. Among the oak and magnolia trees in the churchyard is a natural rock monument with bronze plaques on either side. One of the tablets is inscribed:

In memory of
John Dinkins and John Smith
first deacons of
The Flint Hill Baptist Church

John Dinkins was the first Baptist resident of Mecklenburg County of whom there is any record. Dr. Pritchard, the great-grandson of John Dinkins, wrote in 1896 concerning his great-grandfather. "The first Baptist known in Mecklenburg County was John Dinkins. He was an Irishman, and a man of means, and resided on the Nations Ford Road, half a mile beyond the Mineral Spring on Sugar Creek."

The John Dinkins house still stands in the vicinity of Pineville near the Charlotte city limits, a Federal-style structure that was built for Dinkins on land he acquired in the late 1700's. The house, which has been designated an Historic Site by the Charlotte-Mecklenburg Historic Properties Commission, has an exterior of white clapboard, flanked on each side by tall brick chimneys, and has exquisite interior woodwork. It was to this home that John Dinkins brought the first pastor of the Flint Hill Church. Dr. Pritchard wrote concerning his great-grandfather, "He sent his overseer to Richmond, Va., with a covered wagon, drawn by four horses, and brought to his plantation, on which he had built a parsonage, the Rev. John Rooker, whose family was supported almost entirely by him for some time."

An inscription on the second tablet in the Flint Hill churchyard reads:

In Memory of
ELDER JOHN ROOKER
born in Virginia, March 12, 1755
Came from Warren County, N. C.
to York County, S. C., November 1790
Pastor of Flint Hill Baptist Church
from its organization, May 1, 1792,
until his death, June 24, 1840

Dr. Taylor learned from a sketch written about and by the minister himself that Rev. Rooker was born in Virginia and moved to Bute, now Warren County, North Carolina, about 1775. He was a soldier in the Revolutionary War, later taught school in Warren County, and married Ann Hawkins, daughter of John Hawkins of Warren. Rooker joined the Baptist church of which Elder Thomas

Gardner was pastor and was licensed to preach by that church. Rooker's name is among those in the early records of the Reedy Creek Church in Warren County. From Warren County he moved to the neighborhood where John Dinkins resided. Dr. Taylor thought that Rev. Pritchard was mistaken in thinking that Rooker moved from Richmond, Virginia, to Mecklenburg County, but thought it very probable that it was through the efforts of John Dinkins that the minister was persuaded to settle in that section. This writer thinks that both men may have been correct, since it is possible that Rooker may have made a sojourn in Richmond after he came to North Carolina and before he moved to Flint Hill.

Dr. Taylor described the constitution of the Flint Hill Baptist Church. "Evidently Elder Rooker's purpose in moving was that he might preach the gospel and establish churches in this inviting field; for almost as soon as he had located, he, with the assistance of Elder Abraham Marshall, of Georgia, constituted, on the first day of May, 1792, Flint Hill Church, which, although in York County, South Carolina, is only twelve miles from Charlotte, with which place the Flint Hill neighborhood has always been closely identified. Some of the constituent members of this church moved with Elder Rooker from Warren County, others came from Virginia, and the remainder, like John Dinkins, had for some time resided in that community."

The records of the Flint Hill Baptist Church begin with the institution of the church. "May 1st, 1792. This day, after examination into the faith and order of several members of the Baptist denomination, residing on the Catawba Indians' land and the vicinity thereof, was constituted a Baptist church, by the Rev. Abraham Marshall, minister of the Gospel, of the State of Georgia."

The church entered the Bethel Association, and from the *Association Minutes, 1793–1803*, it is learned that on October 29, 1793, James Fowler and Joseph Camp came by request to the Sugar Creek (Flint Hill) Church and "Set apart by Solemn prayer to God and laying on of hands, John Dinkins Sen. and John Smith Deacons, and John Rooker minister." There were twelve members at that time, including one slave. Other members soon joined the church, shown in the church records to have come from Virginia,

North Carolina, and New York. In March, 1799, two acres of land for the meeting house and burying ground were laid off.

In its early days the Sugar Creek Church was encouraged and helped by the Charleston Baptist Association. According to the association's records, Rev. Rooker, during a long period of his pastorate, was paid a salary of 30 pounds sterling each year by the Charleston Baptist Church to preach to the Catawba Indians. Rev. Rooker was pastor of the Sugar Creek church for 42 years. On an old stone in the Flint Hill cemetery, an inscription reads:

In Memory of
ELDER JOHN ROOKER
who was born on
the 12th of March, 1755
in the State of Virginia,
and departed this life on the
24th of June, 1840,
in the 86th year of his age.
In 1782, he united himself with the
BAPTIST CHURCH
in which charge he remained until the time of his death.
He was a man sound in doctrine
and earnestly contended for the faith once delivered
to the saints, as believed by the
regular Baptists.

During the latter part of his pastorate at Flint Hill, a small number of his congregation helped to spawn a young church in Charlotte of Mecklenburg. Dr. Taylor's paper described the beginning of Baptist work in Charlotte. "Although Flint Hill was from the first a prosperous church, and had labored to establish churches in other communities, yet for forty years no effort seems to have been made to organize a Baptist church in Charlotte. It is altogether likely that Father Rooker occasionally preached there, for Dr. Samuel Fox, a prominent member of Flint Hill Church, had been a resident of Charlotte for some years." In the summer of 1832, a member of the Flint Hill Church who resided within a few miles of Charlotte, Col. Thomas Boyd, with the cooperation of Dr. Fox, extended the invitation to the two young preachers, Furman and Barnes, to hold a revival in Charlotte.

At this time, Rev. James C. Furman was known as the boy preacher; later he was to become the distinguished president of Furman University. In June of 1832 he and Mr. Barnes were conducting a series of meetings in Camden, South Carolina, which were attended by Col. Boyd, who was in Camden on business. At Col. Boyd's persistent urging, the young preachers consented to come to Charlotte to hold a meeting at the close of their work in Camden. Col. Boyd returned to Charlotte to make arrangements for the meeting. The young preachers were to be the guests of Dr. Fox, and the revival services were to be held in a meeting house on a lot owned by the town of Charlotte.

The town to which the preachers were invited was nestled in the center of the Scotch-Irish settlements. It had been named for Queen Charlotte of Mecklenburg, Germany, the wife of King George III of England, when North Carolina was a British colony. Incorporated in 1768 and designated as the county seat of Mecklenburg County in 1774, Charlotte was known before and during the American Revolution as a hotbed of independent patriots, and in years to follow it never lost that characteristic. The provincial town commissioners built a courthouse, stocks, and jail, and laid out the town in half-acre lots.

Charlotte was described by a journalist in the early 1800's as a village with two main dirt roads (which later became Trade and Tryon Streets) intersecting at a place called the Square. In 1832 the town had a population of 300 people and was protected by one law enforcement officer called the "Town Watch." The borough had a newspaper called *The Catawba Journal* and a second publication, the *Miner's and Farmer's Journal*. There were stagecoach services to the east and to the south, a post office, several stores, a saw mill, a flour mill, one fire engine, and one local branch bank. Andrew Jackson, who was born in what was then Mecklenburg County in 1767 and who in his youth was briefly schooled in Charlotte at Liberty Hall, was President of the United States. At this time the nation, comprised of 24 states, had a population of over ten million people, mostly rural, who were in the grip of westward expansion; and Charlotte was a wayside stop on the route to the farther western frontiers of the young country.

The town was an odd mixture of Presbyterian fundamentalism and gold-rush fever. Since the discovery of gold some years before, hundreds of miners, engineers, and fortune hunters had poured into the surrounding area, and Mecklenburg was fast becoming the gold capital of the United States. As taverns flourished, there was a considerable traffic in whiskey, balanced by the Presbyterians with an organization called the "Sons of Temperance."

Although the town was surrounded by churches throughout Mecklenburg County, from the time of its incorporation until 1815, there was no church building or organized church in Charlotte. Concerned by this lack, the town commissioners set aside in that year a parcel of land (now the site of the First Presbyterian Church, bounded by Trade, Church, Sixth, and Poplar Streets) to be used for a church and cemetery. A brick building was begun in 1819 and completed in 1823, with the principal contributors being Presbyterian gentlemen, William Davidson, John Irwin, William Smith, William Carson, and others. The meeting house was dedicated in 1823 and was used as it was intended by the commissioners by all church denominations.

The title to the property was retained by the town authorities, and in 1832 there still remained an uncomfortable debt of $1500 against it from an amount which the commissioners had borrowed from the Charlotte branch of the Bank of Newbern. It was again a Presbyterian, John Irwin, who paid this indebtedness, and in return the deed to the property was given to the people who were to organize the First Presbyterian Church of Charlotte. At the time of the revival led by Furman and Barnes, the church and the lot were still town property, and it was here that Col. Boyd made arrangements for a meeting to be held.

The two young preachers came to Charlotte at a time when revivalism was sweeping the country. The movement, emphasizing individual religious experience, had started decades earlier on the American scene within a population ripe and responsive to the fervent, emotional preaching which erupted among Methodists,

Presbyterians, and Baptists. Called the Great Awakening, the movement spread in the 1700's in New England and through the middle colonies, New Jersey, New York, and Pennsylvania.

Now in the early 1800's a second Great Awakening was reaching the frontiers of North Carolina, South Carolina, Tennessee, Kentucky, and beyond. The revival held in Charlotte in the summer of 1832 was typical of those sweeping the nation and was graphically described in Dr. Taylor's sketch.

"The young preachers came to Charlotte and commenced a meeting which continued for three weeks. At first the meetings were held in the church, but it soon became necessary in order to accommodate the large congregations which attended to erect a stand in the yard. The sittings were constantly enlarged, for the influence of the meeting had gone out through the surrounding country, and thousands came to hear the Word of Life. Many came from twenty to thirty miles in wagons, and tented on the grounds. There were five services each day — sunrise prayer meeting, inquiry meeting at nine o'clock, and preaching at eleven o'clock, after dinner, and in the evening.

"Many were awakened and sought religious conversation with the preachers; many scores, says Dr. Furman, were converted; and Dr. Pritchard observes that 'as many as two hundred people were converted.' Many of the converts joined the Presbyterian and Methodist churches, and the membership of Flint Hill was also increased by the meeting.

"At the close of the meeting some of the converts requested to be baptized then and there. In accordance with this request, just before the departure of the young preachers for their homes in South Carolina, James C. Furman baptized nine persons, chiefly young men. This was the first baptism ever witnessed in Charlotte."

One of the results of the revival meeting was the establishment of the first Baptist church in Charlotte, the Beulah Baptist Church. However, there are conflicting records concerning the date of its institution.

The minutes of the meeting in September, 1874, of the Moriah Baptist Association at Waxhaw Baptist Church, celebrating the association's nineteenth anniversary, give the date for the organization of the Beulah Church as July 6, 1832. The records show that "the

Beulah Church, in Charlotte, North Carolina, constituted the 6th of July, 1832, by Brethren Samuel McCreary and Hugh Quinn," petitioned for membership in the association. "The necessary evidence being furnished that it was constituted on gospel principles, it was unanimously received, and the right hand of fellowship was given the delegates by the moderator." Thomas Mason was the moderator, and Joseph Smith and Joseph P. Pritchard were the delegates. In the report "Abstract of the State of Religion in the Churches, Taken from the Letters," the following paragraph occurs:

"Beulah. This church was received into the association this year. It was constituted on the 6th of July, 1832, by Elders Samuel McCreary and Hugh Quinn, with nine members. Since then 31 have been added and one has died; present number 40. Their supply is Elder John Culpepper, Jun. Preaching 1st and 4th Sundays. They sent $1.00 for the minutes."

This record was made closest to the date of organization, and Marvin Crowe in his history of the First Baptist Church of Charlotte, *A Biography of a Thriving Church*, took it to be correct.

A second date recorded for the institution of Beulah Church is September 6, 1832. C. J. Black in *A Short History of Independence Hill Baptist Church*, reported that the work of Furman resulted in the organization of a Baptist church with nine white members on September 6, 1832, by Revs. Hugh Quinn and Samuel McCreary.

A third date given is September 12, 1832. Carrie L. McLean in her history of First Baptist Church, which was written in 1916, referred to a journal kept by Col. Thomas Boyd. She wrote, "It was on Sept. 12, 1832, that the Beulah Baptist Church was constituted in Charlotte, and the first Lord's Supper by the Baptists was celebrated in Col. Boyd's house, preceded by a conference." Col. Boyd's account was the testimony of an eye-witness to an event which occurred in his own house.

A fourth date given is 1833, and this date, although probably not the original date, is the one inscribed on the corner stone of the old First Baptist Church building on North Tryon Street.

Dr. Taylor wrote concerning the results of the Furman and Barnes revival,

"In consequence of this great revival, a Baptist church in Charlotte became not only a probability, but a necessity. Therefore, in June, 1833, ten persons were dismissed from Flint Hill Church for the purpose of organizing a Baptist Church. The names of these constituent members were Joseph Smith, Ephraim Bound, Joseph P. Pritchard, Eliza H. Pritchard, Margaret J. Henderson, Samuel W. Fox, Cynthia E. Fox, Thomas Boyd, Susannah Boyd, and W. C. Dyser. This church erected a small frame building on Third Street, near the gas works. The frame of this building was still standing in 1891."

Dr. Taylor's statement is corroborated by the minutes of Charlotte Baptist Church, under the date of August 28, 1878: "Brother Graham, on behalf of Rev. J. P. Pritchard, presented to the church the original letter of dismission from the Sugar Creek Baptist Church granted to J. Smith, Wm. C. Dyser, Eph Bound, Joseph P. Pritchard, Elizabeth Pritchard, Margaret J. Henderson, S. W. Fox, Cynthia Fox, Thos. Boyd, and Susannah Boyd on the 9th of June, 1833, to form a Baptist church at Charlotte."

Perhaps all these dates have some basis in fact. Perhaps the church was hard a-borning and struggled to survive. Without doubt the members from the Flint Hill Baptist Church were also the original group who banded together in 1832. These events were the beginning of the church which was to spawn no less than 76 congregations in Charlotte and Mecklenburg. The name chosen for it, Beulah, means "a blest and happy land," and one must surmise that its founders were aware of the verse in Isaiah, "Thy land shall be called Beulah: for the Lord delighteth in thee."

| Chapter 2 | # The Early Struggles of Beulah, 1833–1857 |

During the first 38 years of its existence, the Beulah Church largely owed its survival to three men. The faith, dedication, and persistence of these three — one a layman, one a missionary, and one a pastor — carried the little church through its first faltering years.

The layman was Colonel Thomas Boyd, who had arranged the Furman and Barnes revival, who had offered his home as a meeting place for the institution of the church, and who for 22 years nurtured it as his child.

After its institution, the church secured a lot of nearly an acre of land on the northwest corner of Third and College streets, shown in the Mecklenburg Registry to have been deeded on February 10, 1833, by the Commissioners of Charlotte to Dr. Fox, Joseph Smith, and Joseph P. Pritchard, trustees of the Charlotte Baptist Church, for the consideration of $10. This location, now occupied by the Southern National Center, is two blocks from the present First Baptist Church building on South Davidson Street. The early site was chosen by the Beulah Church because there was a large spring on the lot. The congregation erected a little frame building on a rock foundation, with two small dressing rooms and a baptistry outside and behind the church. The baptistry was supplied by water from the spring.

How long the Beulah Church occupied this building is not known. Nor are there other than scant records concerning the early pastors of the church. Dr. Taylor recounted in his paper: "It is impossible to ascertain who served this church as pastor, but I remember to have heard in my boyhood the older citizens of Charlotte speak of Elder Rooker as a Baptist preacher, who formerly

13

preached in the town, and who was generally the guest of Dr. Samuel Fox or Col. Boyd, both of whom were influential Baptists and prominent citizens. It is, therefore, probable that for a time Elder Rooker divided his pastoral labors between this church and Flint Hill."

There are a few records concerning later preachers. D. A. Thompkins in his *History of Mecklenburg County* wrote that Mr. Barnes of the Baptist denomination was preaching in Charlotte in 1833, and he, Culpepper, and Wait preached in 1834. One can only speculate whether this was the same Mr. Barnes who led in the 1832 revival. Culpepper and Wait were prominent North Carolina Baptists. Minutes or other records of the Beulah Church from its organization to 1856 have never been located, but the minutes of the Moriah Baptist Association of South Carolina contain some information about the church. In 1834 the Beulah Church joined the Moriah Association, which included churches in a wide area of South Carolina and a few in North Carolina. The association minutes for that year list Elder John Culpepper, Jr., as supply pastor. Concerning Culpepper, Dr. C. B. Williams in his *History of Baptists in North Carolina* wrote: "Eighteen hundred thirty four was a most prosperous year in state missions. John Culpepper, in his seventieth year, in his sulky, visited in 30 counties including Mecklenburg and Cabarrus." Culpepper apparently visited his son and preached in Charlotte.

In 1836, according to the Moriah Association minutes, J. Thomas was pastor of the Beulah Church, preaching on the first and third Sundays of each month. There were four baptisms that year and a total of forty members reported. The 1838 minutes contain this paragraph:

"The committee on Requests and Queries beg leave to make the following report: Resolved, that we recommend that the association appoint a committee to visit the Beulah Church whose duty it shall be to endeavor to reconcile the party who professes to be grieved in the said church." The treasurer of the Home Mission Board of the Moriah Association reported "received from Elder W. Nolen from the Beulah Church, $5.00." There were six baptisms reported and a total of forty members. Elder W. Nolen was preaching on the first and third Sundays. Two years later, both W. Nolen and J. P. Pritchard were named as pastors in the associational minutes of 1840. Apparently Nolen resigned and Pritchard was called during the year. There was only one baptism and the membership had been reduced from 40 to 24. J. P. Pritchard was the grandson of John Dinkins, the first Baptist in Mecklenburg.

There are two accounts of Pritchard's changing theological beliefs. Pritchard and his wife were converted during the Furman and Barnes revival and were among the 36 persons joining the group of Presbyterians who on the fourth Sabbath in August of 1832 organized the First Presbyterian Church of Charlotte. The 1833 records of that church provide interesting information about Joseph P. and Eliza Pritchard. "Jos. P. Pritchard, having fallen into antinomian views of doctrine, and not being able to reconcile the baptism of infants with foreordination, left us and joined the Baptists." The Pritchards joined the Flint Hill Baptist Church and were listed among the members of that church who were granted letters of dismissal to become a part of the Beulah Church.

While pastor of the Beulah Church, Pritchard also served as pastor of the Flint Hill Church and the Rocky River Church in the present Hopewell community. Another account of his doctrinal views is given by C. J. Black in *A Short History of Independence Hill Baptist Church*: "Pritchard imbibed some very dangerous doctrine during his last days, and this may account for the decline of this noble church. They say that he accepted the hardshell creed and possibly a part of the Adventist faith: anyway, it ruined him in this section." Historian John Brevard Alexander wrote of Rev. Joe Pritchard, "I will mention the fact that he was a great believer in Millerism; he afterwards moved west."

The close relationship between the Beulah Church and the Flint Hill Church continued for several years. Every spring and fall the Baptists of Charlotte would go to Flint Hill for communion. One such day is described by Col. Boyd in his diary: "May 14, 1843 — This day my wife and self saw three baptized at Flint Hill at 9:30 o'clock. Came up to house at 11:00. Old Bro. Posy preached almost two hours. Bro. Thomason followed nearly one hour. Twenty minutes intermission. Bro. Pritchard about one hour and a half — one of his great visions. Communion then by Bros. Stricklen and Posy to a large number of members. All from our Charlotte church communed; all in peace. My wife and self left Flint Hill for Charlotte at five o'clock; got home and ate supper by nine."

Col. Boyd's reference to "all in peace" may have been related to the dissension earlier reported to have been present among some of the members of the Beulah Church. This problem among others plagued the church during the early years. Dr. Taylor wrote: "Deaths and removals greatly weakened the church, and a want of harmony between two prominent families resulted in its dormancy." Dr. Pritchard was succeeded as pastor by Elder James M. Thomas, who is said to have been a hindrance rather than a help to the cause. This situation, together with the controversial feelings caused by a Christmas ball held at the home of one of the leading members (which the pastor and others tried in many ways but in vain to prevent) caused the dissensions referred to by Dr. Taylor, — even though the member himself claimed not even to have heard the fiddle. The journal of Col. Boyd told of trials through which the little church had to pass, many of which vexed his righteous soul.

For many years the church was small, never reaching a membership of 50 during the first 25 years of its existence. In 1842 there were only eleven white members, and every Sunday afternoon at two o'clock Col. Boyd and Joseph Smith met with the black members. During the years when the church had no regular preaching, Col. Boyd faithfully made reports to the Moriah Association and attended the associational meetings. When the church was twelve years old, he, then 67 years of age, rode (in October, 1844) 34 miles each way to attend the Association. The letter he took is as follows:

"Charlotte Beulah Baptist Church sends greetings to the Moriah Association at Meadow Brush:

"Dear Brethren:

"We once more meet you in your deliberations with our brethren Joseph Smith and Thomas Boyd. We have nothing to say to you. We are all at peace. We have had no preaching for some months. Dear Brethren, pray for us, that the Lord will send someone to go in and out before us. The state of our church is thus: Baptized 1; Received by letter, none; Excommunicated, none; Dead, none; Dismissed, 3; Whole number, 39. (This number included about 30 colored members.) We send $1.00 for minutes."

For the ten years from 1845 through 1854, there exist only five dated records concerning the Beulah Church. A copy of the Moriah Associational Minutes in the archives of the American Baptist Historical Society, Chester, Pennsylvania, for 1845, reports that the Beulah Church baptized three and was represented in the association by T. Boyd. In 1847 the report to the association showed six white and nineteen black members. Col. Boyd at age 70 went 70 miles "with his carryall" to the association. At his invitation, the association for the next year was to meet with the Beulah Church in Charlotte.

In December, 1850, Col. Boyd wrote that for nearly seven years the church had held no regular preaching. It was said by those who had some recollections of that time that once in a while someone would happen along and there would be preaching in the courthouse, which stood where the Selwyn Hotel was later built, on the northeast corner of Trade and Church streets. Often these itinerant preachers, wearing blue trousers and carrying their saddlebags, were made fun of by the more cultured people; but however unlettered some of them may have been, they kept the Baptist cause from entirely dying out in the community during these years when Baptists in Charlotte were but a feeble number.

The Moriah Association minutes for 1853 report Joseph Smith as pastor of the Beulah church, but nothing further is recorded about his pastorate. The record of the Moriah Association meeting with Providence Church, Lancaster District, South Carolina, September 30, 1854, shows Beulah as not represented by messengers or letter, but as sending fifty cents for the minutes. There are no further records concerning Col. Thomas Boyd, the man who did the most to keep the Baptist faith alive in Charlotte.

After this faithful layman came a faithful missionary. Although the Baptist church in Charlotte was dormant, there were a number of loyal Baptists still counting themselves as church members who were only waiting for the Lord to send them a leader. Historian Alexander lists among the prominent members of the Baptist church during this time Dr. Steven Fox, Dr. Torrence, William Cook, Mr. Boon (who kept a shoe store), Benjamin Smith, and Leonard Smith, with their families. Then the answer to Beulah's prayers came from the North Carolina State Convention, which

sent R. B. Jones from the Convention to set up a Baptist mission
in Charlotte and to revive the Beulah Church. When the Convention sent Jones to Charlotte, it was fulfilling the purpose for which
it had been organized.

Its organization had come on a spring day in 1830 in Greenville,
North Carolina, when 14 delegates from across the state formed the
North Carolina Baptist State Convention for the expressed objective "to see Baptist churches in places where they are not, and to
see all the churches come under the superintendence of a faithful
and successful ministry." The Convention began with more than
15,000 members in 272 churches, but more churches were needed
in the rapidly growing state. By 1854 the Committee on Church
Extension realized the "hopelessness of effecting permanent good
in our towns and villages without a church edifice." It urged the
Convention to organize a Church Extension Society to assist in
building village churches. Another committee recommended that
the Convention maintain stations in Greensboro, Salisbury, Wades-
boro, Goldsboro, Charlotte, Carthage, Lumberton, and Washington. The board employed six missionaries, one of whom was R. B.
Jones, under whose leadership the Baptist church in Charlotte was
revived. The congregation met for worship services in the courthouse on the corner of West Trade and Church streets. This building was a two-story red brick structure with white columns and
with an outside white marble double staircase leading to the second floor. It was available to the citizens of the town for public
meetings.

Dr. Taylor wrote about the beginning of Rev. Jones's work in
Charlotte:

"In 1853 or 1854 Rev. R. B. Jones, a missionary of the North
Carolina Baptist State Convention, established a mission in Charlotte. He obtained permission to preach in the courthouse and
commenced work. He did not find the way of a Baptist preacher in
Charlotte strewn with flowers. The history of the late church was
not at all helpful to him, the baser sort, of course, were not friendly
to any preacher of the gospel, and the other denominations had but
scant welcome for an aggressive Baptist preacher like R. B. Jones.
One incident will suffice to show the annoyances with which he had
to contend.

"As has already been stated, the Baptists had secured permission to hold services in the courthouse, and everything moved smoothly for a time; but one Sunday morning when Jones and his congregation appeared at the courthouse door they found themselves locked out. Old blind Dick, the janitor, was found; but he said the key had been taken from him the night before, by whom, and for what reason, he would not say. Mr. Jones was equal to the occasion. He mounted a goods box and preached to the people in the court yard. This novel way of preaching attracted the attention of those who passed by, many of whom stopped to hear him, and as a result he had a larger audience than he would have had if the key had not been lost. This evidently did not please those through whose influence he had been shut out, for at the next appointment he found an open door."

To revive the dormant Beulah Church, Rev. Jones with the assistance of Dr. Thomas H. Pritchard reorganized the church the first Sunday in January, 1855, calling it the Beulah Baptist Church of Christ. Dr. Pritchard was the son of Joseph P. Pritchard, who was a charter member of the original church in Charlotte.

After reorganization, the church secured a lot on the corner of Seventh and Brevard streets on which it erected a neat brick building at a cost of about $1,800. T. J. Taylor wrote that Mayor Benjamin Morrow "kindly gave the church the lot." The Mecklenburg Registry of Deeds, however, records a duplicate deed in which Major Benjamin Morrow sold the lot to the church for $300. This is the duplicate deed which the church later went to great lengths to acquire after the original deed was lost. Matthew A. Edwards, a wealthy member of the Flint Hill Church, who resided some four miles east of Charlotte, is credited with making the largest contribution to the building.

Rev. Jones used the occasion of the associational meeting to promote the needs of the new church building. On October 5, 1855, he was cordially received at the fortieth anniversary session of the Moriah Baptist Association meeting with Meadow Branch Church in Union County and preached one of the missionary sermons. The report of the Committee on Requests and Queries included the following paragraph:

"We see in the letter from Beulah Church that an appeal is made to our charity, to aid in building their new house of worship, that it may, as near as possible, compete with those of other denominations. We, therefore, hope that a response will be made, by as liberal a contribution as may be in our power, both to building their house of worship, and to the support of the missionary who labors there."

The Home Mission Board of the association reported a contribution of $15.00 paid to the Charlotte Mission. The associational minutes show that R. B. Jones was its pastor, that preaching occurred on the first Sunday of each month, that three were baptized, five received by letter, making a total of 35 white members. $1.00 was sent for the minutes, $2.20 for home missions, and $3.75 for state missions.

The new building was occupied on September 7, 1856, and at this point there are complete records of the church conferences in the Church Minutes Book for the years from 1856 to 1890. The events on the day the congregation entered the new building are given in graphic detail. For two days the church met and achieved the dissolution of the Beulah Church and the organization of the Charlotte Baptist Church of Christ. The first day of meetings was given to preaching. The minutes read:

"Beulah Baptist Church of Christ

at Charlotte, N. C.

Sabbath, Sept. 7, 1856

"This morning at half past 10 o'clock our new House of Worship was opened. Reading of the scriptures and sermon by Elder P. Nicholson from John IV 23. The house was completely filled and the audience gave serious attention. Elder R. B. Jones, missionary of the North Carolina Baptist State Convention, who commenced laboring in this place the first sabbath in January, 1855, preached in the evening at 2 o'clock. Elder P. Nicholson preached again at night."

This was the last regular service of the Beulah Baptist Church under that name, and on the next morning the church sat in business session for the purpose of dissolving itself. The entry in the church book gives an honest appraisal of the reasons for disbanding. The congregation was aided by an invited group of Baptist ministers from surrounding areas.

"Monday Morning, Sept. 8, 1856

"The church met in their House of Worship at 9 o'clock. Elder R. B. Jones offered prayer. The church then sat in conference, Elder Jones in the chair. Visiting brethren were invited to seats with us. Elder P. Nicholson, and Brethren Richard Smith, Richard Kendrick and J. R. Garrison and M. Edwards of Sugar Creek Baptist Church, James Robison of Long Creek Baptist Church, T. Robison and A. Robison of Salem Baptist Church, James Hawkins and Jacob Hawkins of Bruington Baptist Church, were present and accepted the invitation.

"The moderator then rose and briefly stated the object of the meeting. Wherefore Bro. J. W. Gibson offered the following preamble and resolution:

"Whereas in the providence of God we have been enabled to erect a new House of Worship to the honor of his name, and whereas internal difficulties have existed that have marred our peace and prosperity, therefore,

"Resolved that we the Beulah Baptist Church of Christ at Charlotte be dissolved, and invite a Presbytery to constitute us into a new organization to be called the Charlotte Baptist Church of Christ, — the said new organization to have and to hold the property belonging to the Beulah Baptist Church of Christ at Charlotte, N. C.

"That the Moderator appoint a Committee to prepare a Covenant Letter and arrange business necessary for our organization this evening.

"Resolved furthermore that those members who were excluded in the aforementioned difficulties, and have since their exclusion maintained a Christian character may be restored, on application to the Charlotte Baptist Church, to fellowship therein.

"On motion of Bro. Joseph Smith the above resolution was unanimously adopted. The Moderator appointed a committee to prepare the Covenant Letter and arrange business for the evening, consisting of Elder P. Nicholson and Deacons J. R. Garrison and T. Robison.

"On motion of Bro. J. W. Gibson the Moderator was added to the committee. After singing a hymn, the church adjourned to meet at three o'clock this evening."

"Monday evening, Sept. 8, 1856

"The church met according to adjournment. A presbytery was formed consisting of Elders P. Nicholson, J. M. Garrison, R. B. Jones and Deacons J. R. Garrison and Thompson Robinson.

"Elder Nicholson read the Declaration of Faith and Covenant Letter, which were unanimously adopted by the church. After the singing of an appropriate hymn and prayer by Elder R. B. Jones, the members who formerly composed the Beulah Baptist Church of Christ were now by their desire pronounced by the presbytery, the Charlotte Baptist Church of Christ.

"On behalf of the presbytery, Elder Jones gave the church the right hand of fellowship. Elder Nicholson delivered the charge.

"The Charlotte Baptist Church then sat in conference and elected Jno. W. Gibson their deacon, whom they set before the presbytery for ordination. Elder J. M. Garrison offered the ordination prayer. Elder Jones delivered the charge. The church then appointed Matthew Edwards and Elder Robert B. Jones their trustees and requested Elder Jones to write up the proceedings of their meetings and act as church clerk pro tem.

"Monday, Elder Nicholson preached to a large and attentive congregation. Our meeting then closed in consequence of being disappointed in the expectation of having other ministers to labor with us.

(Signed) Robt. B. Jones
Moderator and Clerk Pro Tem"

The church's disappointment was short lived, however, for Elder J. J. James arrived on Tuesday and preached each night until Friday evening. The first prayer meeting was held in the church on Tuesday evening. A Sunday school was organized the third Sunday morning in September. All these were firsts in the eventful month of September, 1856. The charter members of the church are listed in the roll book by sex and by race:

WHITE MALE MEMBERS

Jasper Smith	Marcus F. Clark
John W. Gibson	R. N. Carter
J. D. Boyd	

WHITE FEMALE MEMBERS

Eliza M. Springs   Mrs. Asa George
Catherine Warlick   Altany Boyd
Minerva Stewart

COLORED MALE MEMBERS

Jack, servant of Taylor   Jim, servant of Phifer
Moses, servant of Grier   Solomon, servant of Pharris
Bob, servant of Elms   George, servant of Elms

COLORED FEMALE MEMBERS

Peggy, servant of Jenkins   Eady, servant of Strange
Cynthia, servant of Caldwell   Alsey, servant of Cook
Dinah, servant of Hampton   ——, servant of Williamson
Rose, servant of Brem   Charlotte, servant of Boyd
Mary, servant of Boyd   Maria, servant of Smith
Nellie, servant of Fox   Nancy, servant of Elms
Maria, servant of Edwards

The servants of many people who were not themselves members of the church were included in its membership. Slaves were required to have the permission of their owners to become church members. The first members to be received by letter were slaves, Zacheus and wife Lavinia, servants of Rev. Dr. Lacy, from the Raleigh Baptist Church. On the first Sabbath in October in the evening, a conference was held with the colored members. "Made inquiry into the standing of the membership of the Beulah Church. The names of those in good standing were enrolled on the New Book of the Charlotte Baptist Church. Peggy, servant of Dr. Graham, was restored to the fellowship of this church."

The Baptists in Charlotte, as elsewhere, were aware of their distinctiveness as a group. Their beliefs were set forth in the Declaration of Faith, which the Charlotte Baptist Church agreed to, on September 8, 1856. The Declaration of Faith is given here in an abbreviated form. Its full text appears in the Appendix of this book.

DECLARATION OF FAITH

I. We believe the Holy Bible was written by men divinely inspired, that it has God for its author, salvation for its end, and truth without any mixture of error for its matter.

II. That there is one, and only one, true and living God, revealed in the Father, the Son, and the Holy Ghost.

III. That man was created in a state of holiness, but by voluntary transgression fell from that holy and happy state; in consequence of which all men are now sinners.

IV. That the salvation of sinners is wholly of grace, through the Son of God, who made atonement for our sins by His death, being risen from the dead.

V. That Christ bestows justification, consisting of the pardon of sin and the promise of eternal life; that it is bestowed not in consideration of any works of righteousness which we have done, but solely through His own redemption and righteousness.

VI. That the blessings of salvation are made free to all by the gospel.

VII. That in order to be saved we must be regenerated, or born again, by the power of the Holy Spirit.

VIII. That election is the gracious purpose of God, perfectly consistent with the free agency of man.

IX. That real believers endure unto the end; that a special providence watches over their welfare.

X. That a visible church of Christ is a congregation of baptized believers, observing the ordinances of Christ; that its officers are bishops or pastors and deacons.

XI. That Christian baptism is the immersion of a believer in water to show forth in a solemn and beautiful emblem our faith in a crucified, buried and risen Savior; that it is prerequisite to church membership, and to the Lord's Supper, in which the members of the church by the use of bread and wine are to commemorate together the dying love of Christ, preceded always by a solemn self-examination.

While the Declaration of Faith set forth the doctrinal beliefs of the church, the Church Covenant had a different purpose. It was to show how church members should act toward each other, walking in brotherly love and exercising charity and helpfulness. The Covenant stressed the importance of an upright life lived in the spirit of meekness for others, believers and unbelievers, to see and respect. It is given here in full as it was adopted by the Charlotte Baptist Church on September 8, 1856.

CHURCH COVENANT

Having been as we trust brought by divine grace to embrace the Lord Jesus Christ, and to give up ourselves wholly to Him, we do now solemnly and joyfully covenant with each other to walk together with Him in brotherly love, to His glory, as our common Lord.

We do therefore in His strength engage that we will exercise a mutual care as members one of another to promote the growth of the whole body in Christian knowledge, holiness, and comfort; to the end that we may stand perfect in all the will of God.

That to promote and secure this object, we will uphold the public worship of God and the ordinances of His house; and hold constant communion with each other therein; that we will cheerfully contribute of our property for the support of the poor, and for the maintenance of the faithful ministry of the gospel among us.

That we will not omit closet and family religion at home, nor allow ourselves to fall into the too common neglect of the great duty of religiously training up our children, and those under our care, with a view to the service of Christ, and the enjoyment of heaven.

That we walk circumspectly in the world that we may win souls; remembering that God has not given us the spirit of fear but of power, and of love, and a sound mind; that we are the light of the world and the salt of the earth, and that a city set upon a hill can not be hid.

That we will frequently exhort, and, if occasion require, admonish one another according to the gospel of Matthew, Chapter 18, in the spirit of meekness; considering ourselves lest we also be tempted, and that in baptism we have been buried with Christ, and raised again, so there is on us a special obligation henceforth to walk in newness of life.

And may the God of Peace who brought again from the dead our Lord Jesus, that great Shepherd of the sheep, through the blood of the everlasting covenant, make us perfect in every good work to do His will, working in us that which is well pleasing in His sight through Jesus Christ; to whom be glory forever and ever. Amen.

The first mention of an association in the minutes-book was dated September 5, 1857, when R. B. Jones and W. A. Cook were

appointed as delegates. The minutes of the Brown Creek Association, which met at Mt. Olive Church in Anson County on October
9 through 12, 1857, include the following paragraph: "The church
at Charlotte, being newly constituted, presented a letter asking for
admission into the association. After reading before the association
a Declaration of the Principles on which it was organized, it was
admitted." The Brown Creek Association had been organized by
Faulk's, Monroe, and Mt. Olive churches in 1854 and was the first
North Carolina association with which the Charlotte church was
affiliated.

Elder R. B. Jones began his work in Charlotte as a missionary
from the North Carolina Baptist Convention, but shortly after the
church's reorganization in January, 1857, he began work as a full-
time pastor, no longer sharing his efforts in other mission duties.
The following excerpts from the minutes of the church conferences
during his pastorate are presented here as items of interest, quaint-
ness, and importance to the life of the church at that time. They
were entered in the church-book variously by R. B. Jones, clerk pro
tem, L. H. Smith, clerk, and R. B. Jones, moderator.

"Sabbath Evening, Oct. 18, 1856. The church celebrated the Lord's
Supper. At 2 o'clock collected for contingent expenses $10.40."

"Saturday Evening, Nov. 1, 1856. Bro. L. H. Smith, and Bro. Jones
Moody and wife Catherine Moody presented letters of dismission
from Sugar Creek Baptist Church . . . Bro. Smith was appointed Clerk
of the Church."

"Sabbath Evening 3½ o'clock. The colored members sat in conference.
On motion Sophia, servant of Mr. Irwin, was restored to the fellowship
of the church. A collection was taken up for contingent expenses
amounting to $1.75, and Bro. Zacheus Lacy appointed treasurer."

"Saturday night the church met in a Prayer Meeting."

"December 6, 1856. After sermon by the Pastor, sat in conference.
Sister Eliza Dodge was received on a letter of dismission from Broad
St. Church, Philadelphia. The church was in peace and harmony."

"Sat. night before the first Sabbath, January, 1857. At this time
Elder R. B. Jones commenced his pastoral labors with us, devoting the
whole of his time to this church."

"Sat. Evening, Jan'y 10, 1857. Sermon by L. M. Berry, Agent of the
Domestic Mission Board, SBC. Bro. Jones then presented Rules of
Order for the church which were read and adopted, and will be found
_____. (The Rules of Order, sometimes re-
ferred to as the Church Manual or the Rules of Decorum, were never

recorded in the church book as intended.) A committee consisting of Brethren Cook and Robison was appointed to have some work done on the bell causing it to ring better."

"Feb. 2, 1857. T. Robison and W. A. Cook committee to have the bell fixed, owing to the inclemency of the weather had failed to discharge their duty, and were continued."

"Sat. before first Sabbath in March 1857. The committee appointed to procure the services of a sexton reported that they had employed Anthony, servant of Leroy Springs, at $2.50 a month. Brethren Cook and Robison were continued as the committee to have the Bell better fixed."

"First Sabbath evening, 3 o'clock, March 1857. Met in conference with the colored church. Junius, servant of Leroy Springs, was received for Baptism on the relation of his Christian experience. Baptism deferred until permission is obtained from his master, who is now absent."

"March 23, 1857. Today at 9 o'clock AM our Deacon, Bro. John W. Gibson, died of Pneumonia. His death was a triumphant one. On the 24th, he was conveyed to the meeting house where the pastor preached his funeral. Text John 12:24. A large concourse was present. He was buried with honors of Masonry." (After the death of Gibson, the church was without a deacon for more than a year.)

"Sunday evening April 4, 1857. George, servant of Elms, was excluded for theft."

"Friday night, April 2, 1857. Bro. George Bradford, Agent for Foreign Missions, was with us and preached. Sunday evening April 26th. Bro. Bradford preached his last sermon for us on Sunday evening." He had preached daily from April 2 to April 26, and was assisted by Bro. Nicholson. Several members were added to the church. "He received as Agent for the Southern Board of Foreign Missions in cash $50."

"Oct. 15, 1857. The case of Mr. C——— was reported to the church. C——— being notoriously guilty of drunkenness and profanity, on motion was unanimously excluded from the fellowship of this church."

"Sabbath Nov. 15, 1857. The pastor announced his determination to resign his position as Pastor for the purpose of going to Wake Forest College. Requested him to correspond with the Board relative to getting some one to take his place."

"Friday evening Dec. 4, 1857. The church met at a called meeting in the House of Worship at 3½ o'clock. A communication was read from the Corresponding Secretary of the North Carolina Baptist State Convention, suggesting the name of Elder R. H. Griffith as Bro. Jones' successor, and offering the sum of $400 a year as his salary from them, and requesting the Pastor to write to Elder Griffith immediately."

The final entry in the church book with Rev. Jones as Moderator was made on the Sabbath, December 14, 1857. It read:

"Elder T. W. Tobey from Yancyville commenced preaching for us on Wednesday. Today we celebrated the Lord's Supper, Bro. Tobey assisting our Pastor. In the evening the colored church had communion supper. The Pastor preached the funeral of Sister Alsey Cook, servant of Bro. W. A. Cook. After communion four servants of Mr. J. J. Blackwood, viz: Charles, Clarissa, Fanny, and Sarah, presented letters from the Thankful Baptist Church, Augusta, and were received into the fellowship of this church."

During the pastorate of Rev. Jones, there was an increase in the membership from 29 to 53. T. J. Taylor quoted member William Boyd as saying, "The Convention never sent out a truer or more faithful preacher than R. B. Jones, in whose hands and labors Baptist doctrines and practices could not suffer." Rev. Jones left Charlotte on January 1, 1858 to enter Wake Forest College.

Chapter 3 | The Charlotte Baptist Church of Christ, 1858–1869

The first regularly called pastor of the Charlotte Baptist Church of Christ was Rev. Richard H. Griffith, who ably carried on the work begun by Col. Thomas Boyd and Elder R. B. Jones. Rev. Griffith sustained the Charlotte Church during some of its leanest years. He began his services as pastor on the fifth Lord's Day in January, 1858, coming to Charlotte from Union Mills Baptist Church in Davidson County. He shepherded the little congregation for eleven years, bearing with their inability to pay the salary they promised him. He supplemented his livelihood by teaching school, and in this capacity he was closely associated with a young man who later was to become the chronicler of the Baptists, Dr. T. J. Taylor, whose paper on the Baptists is often quoted in the pages of this history.

With firsthand knowledge, Dr. Taylor assessed the character and abilities of Rev. Griffith: "As a scholar, Dr. Griffith was profound and broad; socially, he was genial, interesting, and pleasing; as a Christian, he was spiritual, devout and consecrated; as a preacher he was able, eloquent, and scriptural; and as a pastor, he was prudent, patient and persevering. This young man of many gifts and attainments came to Charlotte, thoroughly identified himself with the struggling infant church, and for eleven long years laid himself with all his gifts and attainments a willing sacrifice upon the altar for the establishment and building up of the Baptist cause."

Rev. Griffith soon made a favorable impression on the community of Charlotte. That community, as Carrie McLean asserted, was divided into two parts: those who were First Presbyterians and those who were not. That condition was entirely natural, for the

Scotch-Irish Presbyterians had been entrenched in Mecklenburg decades before the Baptists trekked into the county. Dr. Griffith identified not only with the church but also with the town. Dr. Taylor wrote, "When Griffith came to Charlotte, Baptists were regarded as ignorant and unlearned and their preachers received but little attention from other denominations. It was a part of his work to elevate Baptists and Baptist principles in the estimation of that community, and this he faithfully did."

Dr. Taylor told of an incident early in Rev. Griffith's pastorate. "It was perhaps in 1858 that a Union Meeting was conducted by the pastors of the Presbyterian and Methodist churches. Mr. Griffith attended these services, but being as they supposed, only an ignorant Baptist preacher, he was not invited to participate. The meetings had been in progress some time before it was deemed advisable to ask him to preach, but this request was finally made. He took for his text II Kings V:12 'Are not Abana and Pharpar, rivers of Damascus, better than all the waters of Israel? May I not wash in them and be clean? So he turned and went away in a rage.' Imagine such a man as Griffith, with the power of God upon him, preaching to a packed audience in the First Presbyterian Church from such a text as this! The great congregation was held spellbound; the people hung entranced upon the matchless words of truth that fell from the lips of the preacher. The impression was profound and far-reaching. It was a great sermon, and the intelligent people of that cultivated community regarded it as such, and from that day esteemed R. H. Griffith as one of the great preachers of the State. This sermon had the effect of fixing the position of Dr. Griffith in Charlotte, and of increasing the respect of the community for the church that enjoyed the benefits of his ministry."

The entries in the Church Book show the spiritual leadership of Rev. Griffith. "Wednesday night, 17th March 1858. Bro. R. H. Griffith and wife Elizabeth Griffith presented letters of dismission from Union Hill Baptist Church, Davidson County, N. C., and were cordially rec'd into the full fellowship of this church. Bro. R. H. Griffith was then installed Pastor of this church by Bro. Hill of Chester District, S. C."

Perhaps his lectures were too much for some of his listeners, for on April 20, 1859, it was written, "On motion agreed that on Wednesday nights we have Prayer Meetings instead of lectures."

Rev. Griffith continued the close ties with the Brown Creek Association, which had become a strong one. The Brown Creek minutes contain regular reports from the church for the years from 1857 to 1861, and from 1864 to 1865; and, in addition, the Church Book records the election of delegates during some of the missing years. The Charlotte Church retained membership in the Brown Creek Association until 1871, when it asked its delegates to request a "letter of dismission with a view to joining some other association of more convenient access."

The Charlotte Baptist Church maintained close ties with the North Carolina Baptist State Convention. The record states, "Nov. 3, 1858, the Church proceeded to elect members to represent us in the Baptist State Convention, the amt. of funds raised being sufficient to entitle us to five delegates." The next year the Convention met at the Charlotte Church. "1859, Sept. 22. Brethren Boyd, Cook, Boone, and McGaven were appointed a committee to make arrangements for the approaching State Convention. Brother Griffith was added to the committee to make necessary arrangements for warming the church before the meeting of the Convention."

"1859 March. Church met, after singing and prayer by the Pastor, in conference. Read the Declaration of Faith and Church Covenant — and agreed hereafter to have it read regularly, or quarterly during the year."

"1859 Oct. 16. The church observed the ordinance of the Lord's Supper. The exercises were preceded by the giving of the right hand of fellowship to fifteen persons by the Pastor. The Lord grant us many such communion seasons. (Signed RHG)."

In the midst of the Civil War there were held in Charlotte simultaneous revivals by the Baptists, the Methodists, and the Presbyterians. The meeting of the Baptists lasted from October 9 to November 12, 1863, and was led by Rev. William Young, formerly pastor of the Baptist Church in Williamsburg, Virginia, and later Post Chaplain in Petersburg, Virginia.

"Wednesday night, Nov. 12. During this period the Lord graciously revived the church, and many sinners turned to God; about fifty persons were hopefully converted; twenty-three were added to the church, while others joined other denominations; during the progress of our meeting, the Methodists held a series of meetings of much interest, as did also the Presbyterians, and we may humbly trust that God has blessed our labors to such an extent as to extend their influence beyond our own congregation; may the great Head of the Church continue to bless the church and add to her till her numbers shall be greatly multiplied."

The minutes describe the constant struggle to pay the preacher's salary and other expenses.

"Nov. 1858. Bro. Griffith was requested to present to the Board our condition as a church and the propriety of granting us further aid in the support of a Pastor for the next year, — if possible to get the same amount that was given last, which was four hundred dollars."

"1859 January 1st, Saturday. A letter was read from the Corresponding Secretary of the North Carolina Baptist State Convention, appropriating the sum of three hundred dollars to aid us in supporting Bro. R. H. Griffith, Pastor of the church in this place."

"1859 March. Resolved to take up public collection on tomorrow for the purposes of defraying expenses of the church. Appointed Bro. W. A. Cook special agent to make collection for the purpose of paying balance due Bro. Griffith for his services last year. Bro. Boyd moved that some person be appointed to take subscriptions for the support of our Pastor for the present year, which motion was afterwards withdrawn, and resolved to be laid over till next meeting of conference."

"1859 April 2nd. Brethren J. B. F. Boone and W. A. Cook were elected (deacons). Bro. Cook was also Treasurer. Resolved that the plan for securing subscriptions for the support of our pastor be left to the deacons of the church."

"1859 June 4th, Saturday Evening. Reported that the amt. of four hundred dollars was subscribed and paid over, with the exception of fifteen dollars."

"1860 Feb. 15. Bro. Cook read his annual report. His report showed the amount collected and paid to the Pastor $335.00. Still due on subscription list $100.00. Reported that he had rec'd for church expenses $37.50, that he had paid out for same $50.42, leaving a balance due him of $12.92."

"1860 Dec. 8th. Brother Griffith reported concerning assistance from the Board to aid us in supporting our Pastor. Owing to the demand for money, the Treasurer was not able to pay the amount agreed upon this year at present, and could not say what they would do for the next. Resolved that Bro. Wm. Boyd take the list of 1859 and Bro. W. A. Cook to take the list of subscriptions for 1860, and collect them by the 1st of January 1861."

"1861 Nov. 11. Received a communication from our Pastor tendering his resignation as Pastor of the church to take effect at the close of the year. The Treasurer reported that the Pastor's Salary for 1860 was all paid in, and for the present year 1861 there was subscribed $360.00 of which amt. $140.00 had been paid in. The Secretary was requested to furnish delegates to the Convention with a list of all the names of the members of the church, and the means we have for supporting a Pastor in Charlotte." The church refused to accept Griffith's resignation, and he was persuaded to remain.

"1862 Feb. The Treasurer made his report stating that $450 had been paid our Pastor in full for his services for the year 1861, the Pastor paying $50, making the sum of $500, the amount pledged by the church. The church agreed to pledge themselves to give Bro. Griffith $300 for the present year of 1862, and allow him one fourth of his time to supply a church in Iredell County. The Ladies' Sewing Society agreed to pay him $50 in addition to the above salary of $300."

"1867 January 30. Bro. W. A. Cook appointed a committee to settle up bal'ce Pastor's salary for last year. Agree to ask each male member to pay one dollar, and each female to pay fifty cents."

"1867 Dec. 11. Resolved that Bro. Brewer be requested to obtain funds from persons outside the church for the purpose of paying pastor's salary and expenses of the church."

"1868 April 1st. The Deacons report that the amount yet unprovided for Pastor's salary is about $80.00. The Deacons were requested to continue their exertions for the purpose of raising the balance."

"1868 July 29. All agreed and resolved to make every effort to pay our Pastor, Bro. R. H. Griffith, Four Hundred Dollars for the present year 1868, and he to dispense with night services at pleasure."

"1868 December 9. Report that there was a balance due the Pastor of $426.60. To pay this amount there is subscribed $188.50; and a balance due for church expenses of $60.50."

It is well to note that these events took place during the Civil War and the Reconstruction period, when most Southerners were destitute and their Confederate money was worthless. Under these circumstances it is all the more commendable that the Charlotte Church never lost the vision of its responsibility for missions. The church records show that although the church was operating on the most meager of funds and was hard pressed to meet its financial obligations, it gave of what it had to missions.

"April 2, 1859. Agree that the Treasurer of the Missionary Funds be requested to pay over to the Treasurer of the Convention all funds rec'd for missions."

"1858 April 3. The attention of the church was called to the importance of some definite arrangement for the meetings of the colored members, and for holding a monthly concert of prayer for missionaries."

"1860 April 7. Adopted a resolution that the amount collected at our concert meeting be equally distributed betwixt the three objects, Foreign, Domestic, and Indian Missions." Local needs were not neglected.

"1868 February 26. The members of the church were requested to pay ten cents each at every communion season for the benefit of the poor."

There was also concern among the congregation about repairs and improvements needed for its house of worship. In 1858 when the Charlotte Gas Light Company was chartered, the church added gas lighting to its building. "April 3, 1858. On motion Brethren Cook, Boyd, and S. P. Smith (were appointed a) committee to raise money to pay for balance due for the Furnace and Fixtures and for Gas Fixtures lately put into the church. About $100 is necessary." "1858 June, Saturday before the first Lord's day in June. Committee reported that $106 had been procured, and the balance of $30 Brethren Cook, Smith, and others agreed to make up."

There were other items of expense concerning the church building.

"1859 April 17. Bro. Boone (was named to collect funds, and make the necessary arrangements in providing a tent for the benefit of persons to be baptized."

"1860 October 24th. Bro. J. B. F. Boone stated that he had had the church insured and asked the members to pay him the amount, and take up the Policy."

"1864 Oct. 5. On motion, verbal report of Bro. Boyd, chairman of committee in regard to plastering the church was received as satisfactory, and a committee of three was appointed to raise the necessary funds to liquidate the debt, which had been paid by Bro. J. M. Springs."

Of great importance to the Baptist church was the matter of a baptistry.

"1868 Dec. 2. Appointed a Committee to inquire the probable cost of erecting a Baptistry."

"1868 Dec. 30. The probable cost of erecting a Baptistry: estimate was that one in the rear of the pulpit would cost about $600, one inside the house would cost about $300. Next regular meeting to report more specifically as to cost of one inside the house."

"1869 March 3. The committee reported on the construction of the Baptistry, two plans being given. One was that the outside plan was to be 10 x 12 feet, recess back with Baptistry 7 x 9 in the clear, to be brick, the addition be built of wood, all complete to cost $405, or $350 without painting. Plan No. 2: Dressing Room inside, made of plank 10 x 12 high, and use the same floor with steps and pulpit recess back as in plan no. 1. Without painting $250."

Christian churches of that time, Baptist and others, took seriously the matter of Christian discipline, including the procedure for excluding offenders from church membership. At every business conference the Charlotte Church inquired into the state of the members. There follows one such case:

"1859 Feb. 5th. Whereas this church has learned with great sorrow from Mr. C————, member and deacon of this church, that he has been intoxicated, and has also learned from him the circumstances of the case, and his repentance for the same. Therefore it is resolved that this Church do regard a plain case of drunkenness in a member a forfeiture of membership and just cause for exclusion. Resolved that in becoming intoxicated Mr. C———— has forfeited the fellowship of this church. Resolved, however, that in considering the circumstances of the case, and on the ground of the manifest, deep, and voluntary repentance for his offense Mr. C———— be, and hereby is, restored to the fellowship of this church in the spirit of meekness."

Another case of discipline was that of Rose, a slave.

"1859 Feb. 20th. The church met in conference for the benefit of the colored members. A charge was brought against Rose, servant of Dr. M. B. Taylor, for dancing at a party. After some suggestions the case was laid over to a called meeting, as there were but few of the brethren present."

"1859 Feb. 27th. Rose, servant of Dr. M. B. Taylor, on a profession and evidence of repentance for dancing, was excused."

Attendance at church services, meetings, and conferences was considered a matter of serious responsibility.

"1859 December 10th. A committee of young ladies, members of the church, were appointed to give members notice to attend church meetings."

This is the first mention of any role of women in the life of the church.

"1860 Feb. 11. The Committee of Sisters appointed to wait on the male members and request their punctual attendance at church conferences reported through Bro. Boyd that they had attended to that duty. . . . Resolved that seven white male members shall constitute a quorum for the transaction of business."

"1868 April 1st. A resolution was passed that the Treasurer notify those brethren who have been absent for three successive church meetings, to appear at our next regular meeting and render in their excuses for non-attendance — it being contrary to the rules of the church for brethren to be absent for three successive church meetings."

Other items requiring discipline were fighting, selling liquor, and stealing.

"1860 April 7. Bro. S—— reported that he had gotten into two fights. After stating to the church the circumstances, on motion agreed that he was justifiable in all that he had done."

"1861 Nov. 12. One of the brethren stated that Bro. M——, one of the members, was engaged in acting as clerk in a retail liquor shop, a business unbecoming a member of the Baptist Church. A committee consisting of Bros. Wm. Boyd and S. P. Smith were appointed to see him and labor with him in regard to the charge."

"1862 February. In the case of Bro. M—— the report of the Committee was that he is still in the business of selling spirits and said that he intended to continue it. Whereupon the motion being made and seconded, the church withdrew its fellowship."

"1865 January 15. Report of committee on the case of John, servant of Mr. Hutchinson, upon the charge of stealing, was received. Committee finding the charges fully sustained and his acknowledgements not corresponding with the facts connected with the case, in their opinion, deemed him unworthy as a member of the church. On motion he was excluded from the fellowship of the church."

"1868 January 1. Bro. R—— acknowledged to the church that he had been intoxicated, and asked the church to forgive him, which request was granted."

During the Civil War the fighting bypassed Charlotte, but the church was affected in membership and hardship. The church minutes read, "1861 Feb. 10. Passed a resolution to alter the Rules of Order so as to make five male members a quorum, instead of seven, as long as that number constitutes one half of the male members of this church." Associational minutes gave the church membership to be 110 in 1860 and 117 in 1861, these numbers including the resident white males, women, slaves, and white males who were away at war.

When the Confederate Navy Yard was moved from Norfolk to Charlotte, there was an influx of employees and refugees upon the city, to whom the church opened its doors.

"1863 October 30. The Pastor stated that there are brethren and sisters in our town who are members of churches which are now within the lines of the enemy, and that it was desirable to receive the cooperation of the brethren and sisters. Bro. Wm. A. Cook offered the following Preamble and Resolution: Whereas there are in our midst a number of brethren and sisters, members of Baptist Churches in Norfolk and Portsmouth, and whom we desire to unite with us in the duties and privileges of the church, and since it is proper that they should still preserve their relations to their respective churches, — Therefore Resolved that we as a church do cordially invite these Brethren and Sisters to unite with us in the ordinances and privileges of God's house — excepting actual membership — and in labors for our common Lord and the cause of Truth. Which was unanimously adopted.

"Sister Palmer and daughter Miss Jane Palmer, members of the church in Hampton, Va., were unanimously received in the fellowship of the church on evidence of their membership in that church, since the records of that church have been destroyed, the House of Worship destroyed and the church driven away by the public enemy."

Dr. Taylor wrote,

"During the trying period of the Civil War the church experienced many hardships and discouragements. The Sunday school, which was perhaps the most encouraging feature of the church work, was at one time so reduced that there were only one teacher and one scholar; but these two would not let it die, and soon it was reorganized under the superintendency of William Boyd."

The teacher of this class was Miss Jennie Torrence, and the scholar was Taylor himself, as a youth. He wrote in a letter,

"When the Sunday School was reorganized, these two continued, she as the teacher and I as one of her scholars. This noble young woman did more to shape my life than any other person. I would go from her class home to pray."

The Church Book shows that at least three of the members were killed in the war. Sidney Tedder was killed in the battle near

Richmond in July of 1862. Kenny Fullenwider died from wounds received in battle in 1864. Especially poignant was the death of Lieutenant Charles C. Lee, who had been excluded from church membership the year before. The exclusion came after his confession to the membership in church conference that he could not, after much study, bring himself to believe in the deity of Christ nor in the Godhead of the Trinity. When he had been received into the church he had not thought these beliefs to be necessary to church membership. It was a painful experience both to him and to the church, for he was held in high regard and beloved by all. Later having been made a Lieutenant Colonel in the Confederate Army, leading a N. C. regiment in a heroic charge, he was killed in the battle of Seven Pines.

Another death which came at the end of the war and which brought much sorrow to the church was that of Elizabeth A. Griffith, the wife of the pastor. There were no entries made in the church record from March 29, 1865, until November. When the war ended in April, there was looting and turmoil in the city until May 5, when order was restored by the arrival of Federal troops. Five days later on May 10, 1865, Eliza Griffith died, leaving the pastor with two small daughters.

From the institution of the church, the black slaves of the area, always called servants rather than slaves, had been members of the church in good standing. Their masters' permission to join the church was required.

"Feb. 20, 1859. Heard the experience of Robert, servant of R. M. Taylor, which was satisfactory to the church, but he was not received on account of not having the permission of his master. Administered the sacrament to the colored members."

"1859 Feb. 27th. Received Robert, servant of R. M. Taylor, on a profession of his faith in Christ, to the ordinance of Baptism."

At first the Lord's Supper was administered to the colored members separately, but this was soon amended.

"1859 June 12. It has been the practice heretofore that the colored members had the sacrament administered to them at a different time and did not commune with the white members. It was Resolved that hereafter they would all commune together. Also passed a Resolution to change the time of holding communion from the first to the second Lord's day in the month. Dismissed in order."

The black members took it upon themselves to care for their own people.

"1859 July 31st. A proposition from Zaccheus to form among the colored members a Benevolent Society for the relief of the aged and sick of their own members was highly approved of. After remarks from the Pastor on this matter and the duty of giving according to their several ability for the support of the Gospel, on motion adjourned."

Often the slave's master recommended the good character of his servant.

"1860 Oct. Molly, servant of Mr. W. F. Phifer, requested to be rec'd into fellowship of the church. Her master testified to her good character. She stated that she had been up to the time of her leaving the neighborhood, a member in good standing in a Baptist church in Mississippi. On motion Molly was rec'd into the fellowship of the church, the Pastor giving her the right hand of fellowship."

Her master was the Mr. Phifer in whose home on April 20, 1865, the Confederate Cabinet held its last meeting with Jefferson Davis.

The first record of a free Negro coming into the fellowship of the church was made in 1861.

"1861 Sept. 8. Heard a free negro woman, named Caroline Reid relate her experience. When on motion it was resolved to receive her into the fellowship of the church when she shall have been baptized."

At the end of the Civil War when they were no longer slaves, the black members were asked if they wanted to change their church relationships also.

"1866 May 30. Bro. S. M. Springs moved that the colored members hold a meeting for the purpose of consulting them upon the subject of their relation with the white members, whether they desire to form a separate church. Bro. Griffith appointed to lay the matter before them."

"1866 August 8th. Bro. Griffith made his report as to the conference he had held with the colored members, as to their desire to form a separate church. Upon a vote they unanimously desire to remain with the church as heretofore. By vote taken it was decided that the colored members be allowed the privilege of meeting with the church at their regular meetings, and they have the privilege of meeting on Sunday afternoons as heretofore."

From this time the black members were called by their surnames which usually were derived from their former masters.

"1867 July 31. Two colored brethren were rec'd on profession of their faith, viz: Wallace Torrence, and Henry Torrence."

It was almost two years later when the black members formed their own church. Three entries were made in the church book concerning the organization of the black church.

"1867 Dec. 11. Resolved to grant letters of Dismission to the colored members for the purpose of organizing a colored church."

"1868 January 1. Resolved to grant letters of dismission to colored members to all such as are recommended by colored Deacons of the church."

"1868 February 5th. The colored members of the church were under Rev. Mr. Hinton and Rev. R. H. Griffith (Pastor) and the Deacons of the church, in accordance with the letter previously granted, formed into a regular colored Baptist church. The Pastor stated that they have fifty-five recognized members, and were doing as well as could be expected."

A total of 106 colored members were received into the Charlotte Baptist Church in the course of its history. The second Baptist church to be organized in Charlotte was the black church. It secured property on South Church Street and erected a building in 1870.

The first local mission work by the Charlotte Baptist Church of Christ was begun at this time. Dr. Taylor recorded his own part in this enterprise under the tutelage of Rev. Griffith. He wrote:

"With the new life that the city took on after the close of the Civil War, the pastor saw the opportunity for expansion, but owing to the location of the church and the fact that he was engaged in teaching school, it was impossible for him to take advantage of it. Some work was attempted in the southwestern part of the city, and the writer, who was then a student in the High School of which Dr. Griffith and Judge Armistead Burwell were Principals, labored as missionary under the direction of Dr. Griffith. There were many who professed conversion. Very few of them, however, united with the Baptist Church, for at that time the church had not commenced those vigorous missionary movements for which it has been remarkable in later years. It is worthy of note, however, that the Baptists, through the writer (Dr. Taylor), inaugurated the movement in the southwestern part of the city which completely revolutionized that portion of the community. Others soon joined in the work and carried it forward, but it was commenced by the Baptists."

Dr. Griffith resigned from the pastorate of the Charlotte Baptist Church in March, 1869. He had been a faithful pastor and the majority of the church recognized his worth and loved him dearly. There were a few, however, who would not cooperate with him, and thus stood in the way of success. When his resignation was offered, the church by an overwhelming majority refused to accept it, and urged him to remain with them as their pastor. This he kindly but positively declined to do, and the church reluctantly accepted his resignation, and thus, after eleven years, this noble man of God was relieved of the responsibilities that he assumed when he became pastor of the church.

"Two incidents will serve to show the love and esteem in which he was held by the church and the community.

"The first occurred a short time after his resignation had been accepted. Rev. R. H. Moody visited the town and preached on Sunday. It was the regular time for the celebration of the Lord's Supper. At the close of the communion service, the congregation, at the suggestion of the preacher, arose to give to each other the hand of loving fellowship, and as if by one impulse they gathered around their old pastor and pressed his hand with many assurances of love and confidence. It was a scene never to be forgotten by those who witnessed it.

"The other incident revealed his standing in the community outside the church. Without understanding the particulars, it was generally supposed by those without that the church had sacrificed the pastor at the demand of certain unworthy members; therefore, some prominent gentlemen of the city came to Mr. Griffith and offered to put at his disposal the Opera House for holding Sunday services at the same time guaranteeing to him a satisfactory pecuniary support. Never did the true greatness of this man of God more brightly shine than on that occasion. He replied: 'Gentlemen, I appreciate the motives, and with all my heart I thank you for your kind offer, but I have given eleven years of my life to the work of establishing and building up a Baptist church in this city, and I cannot, I will not take a single step that might divide its members or in any way hinder its prosperity.' The esteem that these gentlemen had for him before was increased tenfold by this brave and manly reply."

Dr. Griffith and his two daughters remained as members of the church, and he was often called to act as moderator of the church business conferences. In 1882 the Griffith family moved to Green-

ville, South Carolina, and one of the daughters, Mrs. W. E. Entzminger, became a missionary to Brazil.

Dr. Taylor said of his pastorate:

"Dr. Griffith's pastorate was full of discouragements, trials and hardships; and many of these the pastor was compelled to meet single-
handed. It must be remembered that the young church was composed
for the most part of people of limited means, and the State Convention
was in the infancy of its organized State Mission work. But this self-
sacrificing man of God took the burden upon himself, and by his own
labors supplied the deficiency, and thus continued on the field and
laid that broad and deep foundation on which subsequent pastors have
wisely and successfully built."

Dr. Taylor's reminiscences of those days were happy ones.

"Looking back over those long past days, I see again in memory the
small congregation in the little brick church. There are the Boyds, and
the Boones, and the Cooks and the Johnsons, and the Smiths, and the
Torrences, and others worshipping the Lord in the beauty of holiness.
Up near the pulpit sits the venerable and saintly Mrs. George, and the
devout and consecrated Mrs. Springs. Near the center of the church is
the beautiful and accomplished Miss Jennie Torrence, the ideal Sunday School teacher; and in his accustomed place, leading the singing,
is the big-hearted J. Jackson Blackwood; and in the pulpit the big-
brained, big-hearted, saintly Griffith preaching the Word of Life to his
little band of worshippers."

First Baptist Church, Church Street,
Charleston, South Carolina.
Founded about 1680.

Memorial to
John Rooker, the
founder and first
pastor of the
Flint Hill Church.

Flint Hill Baptist Church,
South Carolina.
Founded in 1792.

The house of John Dinkins, Sr., the first Baptist to live in Mecklenburg County, built on land he acquired in the late 1700s on Nations Ford Road. Designated an Historic Property by the Charlotte-Mecklenburg Historic Properties Commission, the house is Federal style, has exquisite interior woodwork.

Artist's conception of the first building of the Beulah Baptist Church, erected on the northwest corner of College and Third Streets in 1833. Drawing by Paul Wyche.

Rev. R. B. Jones, missionary sent by the North Carolina State Baptist Convention in 1853 to Charlotte to revive the Beulah Church.

Mecklenburg County Courthouse on the northeast corner of Trade and Church Streets, where Rev. R. B. Jones held services for the Baptists from 1853 to 1855, and where the Beulah Church was reorganized.

Church Covenant

Having been as we trust brought by divine grace to embrace the Lord Jesus Christ, and to give up ourselves wholly to Him, we do now solemnly and joyfully covenant with each other, to walk together in Him in brotherly love to His glory, as our Common Lord.

We do therefore in His strength engage, that we will exercise a mutual care as members one of another to promote the growth of the whole body in Christian knowledge, holiness and comfort, to the end, that we may stand perfect in all the will of God.

That to promote and secure this object, we will uphold the public worship of God and the ordinances of His house, and hold constant communion with each other therein. That we will cheerfully contribute of our property for the poor, and for the maintenance of the faithful ministry of the

First page of the hand-written Church Covenant adopted by the Charlotte Baptist Church of Christ in 1856.

Artist's conception of the second building, the Charlotte Baptist Church of Christ, constructed on the southeast corner of Brevard and Seventh Streets in 1856. Drawing by Paul Wyche.

Dr. R. H. Griffith, eloquent pastor from 1858 until 1869, who tended the church and its membership through the dark days of the Civil War.

Rev. J. B. Boone, pastor from 1871 to 1873, who in 1873 established in Charlotte the first graded school in North Carolina.

Rev. Theodore Whitfield (*left*), minister from 1874 to 1881, the first pastor of the church to live in a parsonage and the first to be granted a vacation. Rev. O. F. Gregory (*right*), pastor from 1882 to 1885, under whose leadership the church moved to Tryon Street.

Tryon Street Baptist Church as completed in 1884.

Interior view of the Tryon Street Baptist Church built in 1884.

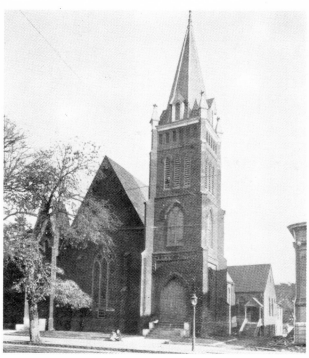

With steeple and Sunday School room added in 1893.

A. G. McManaway, pastor from 1885 to 1892, who gave the church seven years of excellent leadership.

T. H. Pritchard, pastor from 1893 to 1896, a native of Mecklenburg and a well-known leader among North Carolina Baptists.

A. C. Barron, pastor from 1896 to 1905, who established the Charlotte Day Nursery Association for the benefit of children of working mothers.

H. H. Hulten, minister from 1906 to 1912, who at 24 was the youngest pastor ever called to First Baptist, and under whose leadership the large edifice on North Tryon Street was built.

W. M. Vines, minister from 1913 to 1917, the evangelistic pastor who promoted a number of successful church and city-wide revivals.

Architect's drawing of the First Baptist Church, built in 1909.

First Baptist Church and the Andrew Carnegie Free Library, both designed by James McMichael, architect and member of the church.

Interior of the First Baptist Church Sanctuary as completed in 1909.

View of the Sanctuary from the Pulpit, in 1909.

You are most cordially invited
to be present at a

Sociable

to be given by

The Baptist Young People's Union

at the

First Baptist Church
Monday Night, April twenty-third
One thousand nine hundred and six
Eight to ten P.M.
We promise you a pleasant time

Reception Committee

Oates Sprinkle	Bible Class
Misses Bertha Klueppelberg and Lala Kelley	Philethia
C. A. Duckworth and Dabney Yarborough	Baraca
Miss Lochia Lowry and Mrs. Warren Presson	Jr. Philathea
Misses Julia Smith and Neomi Cook	Miss McLean's
Misses Jessie McKamey and Mary Mason	Miss Darsey's
Harold Herndon and Emmett Wishart	B. B. B.
Misses Anna Forbes Liddell and Camile Durham	Mrs. Bryan's
Misses Grace Eddins and Delia Waugh	Mrs. Franklin's

Miss Maud Harrell, Mrs. E. V. Durham, Mrs. J. R. Anderson, Mrs. T. S. Franklin, Mrs. W. C. Dowd, and A. V. Harrell, Joe Pratt and S. F. Haynes.

Invitation to a sociable given by the B. Y. P. U. in 1906. The Baptist Young People's Union was begun at First Baptist prior to 1903.

Dr. Luther Little,
Pastor 1918–1943.

Dr. Little in the 1920s with his Model A Ford.

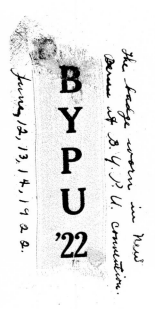

Young members await the train at the Southern Railway Station on West Trade Street to attend the state convention of the Baptist Young People's Union at New Bern in June 1922. Front row left to right are Ethel Vaughan and Ruby Kilgo. Back row left is Sarah Holland.

Garden behind the Carnegie Library and the Education Building of the First Baptist Church, built in 1923.

The Fidelis Class in 1928.

Presidential Prayer

Offered by Dr. Luther Little
Pastor, First Baptist Church
Charlotte, N. C.

◆

On the Occasion of The Green Pastures' Rally
And the Visit of President Franklin D. Roosevelt
September 10, 1936

◆

Thou God *of the universe, and Father of us all, we wait in silence and reverence in Thy beautiful presence. First, we thank Thee for what Thou art. The psalm of praise, which is now singing in our hearts, grows sweeter when we remember that Thou has brought us to this happy occasion. Thou hast brought songs of joy to our hearts by the fellowship and smiles of these many precious guests—men and women gathered here from these many states.*

We are grateful to Thee for our country, its government and its institutions. We hallow Thy name for the great and good men and women who have led us triumphantly thus far. We are grateful to Thee for our citizens in all the walks of life. We are so happy for the certain and ever brightening skies. Thank God for the day-break, and the fleeing shadows.

Especially are we grateful for our human friend and great President, whose gracious presence with us today charms and blesses us with hope and courage. We thank Thee for his good heart, his broad sympathy for suffering humanity, and his tireless toil in our behalf. May Thy unfailing wisdom still be with him. Keep his body, mind, and soul safe—sheltered in Thy love. For the entire nation we pray, and may the blessings of our God be upon all the people here and everywhere.

This prayer we make in our Savior's name. Amen.

First Baptist Church congregation in 1930's. Dr. Luther Little, pastor; Edward E. Rutledge, music director.

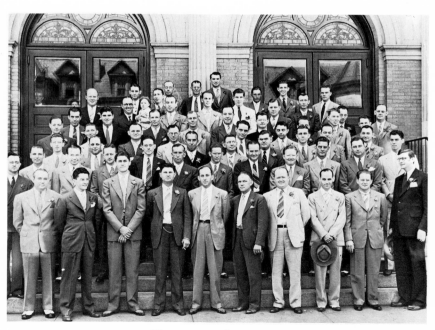

The Berean Class in 1942.

Miss Ree Sheets, church secretary from 1927 until 1944, in the secretary's office.

Church bulletin for December 5, 1943. Dr. Casper C. Warren's first Sunday with First Baptist Church. He served until 1957.

The Service Honor Roll during World War II, on which were listed over 500 names of First Baptist members serving in the armed forces.

The sanctuary as remodelled in 1946. At lower right are Mr. and Mrs. Marvin Crowe. Mr. Crowe was education director and the author of *A Biography of a Thriving Church*, a history of First Baptist.

Adult Sunday School Department in the auditorium of the Education Building.

Dr. Casper C. Warren, always the soul winner, making a call.

Morris Field Baptist Chapel, one of six missions established during Dr. Warren's pastorate.

Commonwealth Recreation Center, on property given to the church in 1948 by H. L. Hopkins and his sisters, Mary, Judith, and Laura.

First Baptist Church choir in 1948, Gertrude Gower director.

Dr. C. C. Warren and church staff. *Front row*: Clarice Price, Mrs. Collier, Ruth T. Sitton, Verl Capps, Dr. Warren, Keener Pharr, Marie Roberts, Elizabeth Hutchens. *Back row*: Carl Whiddon, R. T. Estridge, Robert Rodwell, Penta Burgin.

Meeting of Seasoned Soldiers at Commonwealth Recreation Center.

Education Director Keener Pharr and J. T. Griffis, Superintendent of Standards, displaying Standard Sunday School Banner in May 1959.

Organist Robert Rodwell and young quartet.

Dr. Carl E. Bates,
Pastor 1959–1980.

Vacation Bible School youngsters and teachers in the
1960's.

Rev. Judson Lennon and Harriet Orr Lennon, missionaries to Thailand, who in 1964 while on furlough led the annual youth-sponsored revival. Harriet Lennon grew up in First Baptist and is supported on the mission field by the church.

First Baptist choir caroling on church steps at Christmas time. William Jarvis is choir director.

Former Pastor Warren and Pastor Carl Bates at ground-breaking ceremony on Davidson Street, Easter Sunday, 1971.

Cleve Davenport, beloved janitor of First Baptist since 1944.

Left to right, Attorney Allen Bailey, lay president in 1974 of the North Carolina Baptist Convention; Mrs. Bates; Pastor Carl Bates; Joe Burnette, education director.

First Baptist Church staff: *First row, left to right,* Mary Glover, Zella Oates, Joe Burnette, Betty Mason, Margaret McAlister; *Second row, left to right,* Edna Booker, Mary Ann Lewis, Audrey Metcalfe, Sara Anne Smith, Sarah Clontz, Susan Roberts; *Third row, left to right,* Mrs. Hollifield, Barbara Myers, Janice Broome, Betty Herman, Carol Cone, Pam Jech; *Fourth row, left to right,* Maggie Wright, Elijah Holliday, Roy Gaddy, Tip Cockman, Dennis Bucher, and Marty Gayoso.

The choir of the First Baptist Church in the temporary sanctuary on Davidson Street, with minister of music Dennis Bucher.

First Baptist Church on South Davidson Street in 1981.

Stained-glass window inside the Seventh Street entrance of Spirit Square.

Chapter 4 | The Move to Tryon Street, 1870–1890

As early as 1863, seven years after occupying the meeting house on Seventh and Brevard streets, the members of the Charlotte Baptist Church discussed the need for a new church building. However, four pastorates and 21 years were to elapse before the dream became a reality.

During the tenure of Rev. Robert Griffith, items appeared in the church minutes book indicating that the church was too small and unsuitably located "too far from the center of town!" Two such entries read:

"1863 August. On motion a committee of Bro. Boone, Boyd, and B. R. Smith appointed to inquire into and arrange about fixing the House.

"1863 September 21. Resolved that the Trustees are advised to sell the church, with a view to build another in a more suitable place."

Three years later hope was revived once more and efforts were renewed to secure a lot.

"1866. On motion it was resolved by the church that it is desirable to secure a church lot nearer the centre of town, and to have a new house of worship. Two lots were spoken of as being for sale, and after some deliberation, it was resolved on motion to appoint a committee of three brethren, to be known as the Church Building Committee to whom should be referred and entrusted the matter of securing a lot for a new church."

A year later a committee was appointed to try to buy a lot.

"July 3, 1867. The Committee, appointed to obtain a place for public worship in case the old church should be sold, reported nothing done — prospects rather gloomy. Committee discharged and Bro. Wm. Boyd and S. P. Smith appointed to see the Magistrates of the County in regard

43

to getting the Court House for the purpose of public worship. The Pastor was authorized to advertise the church for sale privately. A committee of three were appointed to buy and obtain a good lot for the purpose of building a church. Com.: S. P. Smith, Wm. Boyd, and the Pastor.

"July 22, 1867. Church held a called meeting on Monday evening. After reading and prayer by the Pastor, proceeded to business. The object of the meeting was explained by the Pastor, as Chairman of the Committee appointed to look out for a lot suitable for building purposes. The Committee reported that a lot nearly opposite the Jail, belonging to Mr. S. A. Harris, mayor of the city, could be obtained for the purpose of building the church. A sense of the church was taken as to the locality and price, and it was unanimously agreed upon as being the most desirable lot that could be obtained. The price of said lot is $2500, upon condition that we pay One Thousand dollars down in cash, and the balance to be paid in one and two year instalments. The church passed a resolution empowering the Trustees to secure the lot if possible, by pledging the property of the church for that purpose, until an opportunity was presented for selling the property."

This lot was not purchased, because the money could not be raised.

The church authorized a committee to attend a sale, December 22, 1870, and to purchase a vacant lot on Tryon Street if sold at a reasonable price, but this lot was not purchased either.

While attempting to buy a lot on which to build a new church, the members were also trying to secure a pastor. After the resignation of Dr. Griffith in 1869, the church remained without a pastor for two years. The deacons served as a pulpit committee, and on August 4, 1869 they reported difficulty in finding anyone to preach. Six times calls were extended to prospective preachers, and six times the preachers declined the invitations. First, the church reelected Dr. Griffith but he declined. Then Brother H. Petty was called June 19, 1870, but he did not accept. S. P. Smith and William Boyd attended the State Convention in Raleigh in November, and, upon their return, reported the names of several ministers whom they thought could be secured. Rev. John Mitchell was called January 1, 1871, at a salary of $700 with the assurance of Dr. Sumner that the Marion Mission Board would pay $300 of that amount. Rev. Mitchell's churches would not release him. Rev. A. J. Emerson was called at a salary of $1,200 with the aid of the Missionary Board at Marion, Alabama. He declined. Rev. William Harrison Williams was called April 5, 1871, but wired "if immediate decision is necessary, I must decline the call." Rev. William Royal, D.D., was called April 19. He visited the church and accepted the call on April 22, but he resigned before moving on the field.

Although the interim between pastorates was generally a time of discouragement, the ladies of the church exuded optimism. The custom of church festivals, with food and entertainment, was now prevalent among the various churches and denominations for the purpose of raising money. Miss McLean wrote that the women worked faithfully, earnestly, and enthusiastically, looking to the day when there should be a new church. Sometimes the festivals lasted for several days and were elaborate affairs. Though Baptist doctrines may not have been to the taste of many, their fried oysters and chicken salad proved most palatable, and at one of these festivals the women of the church made as much as $500. In the minutes the men praised and thanked them.

The financial condition of the church must have reached a low point, indeed, for in August the brethren agreed to act alternately as sexton, each allotment of duty being for two weeks. When cold weather came, they voted to get two new stoves to replace the old stove, and the members were all invited to meet at the church "on Saturday evening at one o'clock, to clean up the church and to place in position the two new stoves." And when Convention time came, an endeavor was made to raise sufficient funds to entitle the church to two delegates, whereas before they had been entitled to five.

Dr. J. B. Boone was elected to serve as pastor of the church on October 1, 1871. The minutes of the church conferences concerning his call are given here in full as illustrative of the methods of the church in acquiring a new pastor — and incidentally, the method of acquiring a new church bell.

"1871 September 17. Church met in called meeting. Bro. Brewer in the chair. It was moved by Bro. Culpepper that Bro. J. H. Mills, of Raleigh be appointed to assist the Committee of our church in obtaining a Pastor. The motion receiving a second, was voted upon and adopted.

"It was then moved by Bro. Boyd to appoint a Committee of four ladies to secure a subscription of amount sufficient to purchase a church bell and expenses of church repairs. The motion receiving a second was voted upon and adopted. Com.: Mrs. Katie Smith, Mrs. William Walker, Miss Eddins, and Miss Annie Cruse.

"1871 October 1. Church met in called meeting. Bro. J. M. Brewer was requested to act as Moderator. The Committee on Pastoral Support begged leave to make their report. Leave being granted, the committee reported, recommending Elder J. B. Boone for Pastor of this Church. The recommendation being seconded, Rev. J. B. Boone was put in nomination. There being no other nominations the members prepared their ballots, and on the votes being cast and counted, it was announced that Elder J. B. Boone was unanimously elected. A Committee of Three (3) was appointed to wait on Bro. Boone, and inform him of his election. Committee consists of Brethren S. P. Smith, D. Austin, and R. Culpepper. Church then adjourned to meet again this evening to receive a report from said committee.

"Afternoon. Church called together. The Committee reported that they had waited on Bro. Boone, and he accepted the call of the church. The church pledged to Bro. Boone a salary of $60 per month, as a minimum amount, commencing from this date. It was then moved and seconded that the Committee on Pastoral Support be discharged from further duty. Adopted. Moved that the committee appointed to wait on Bro. Boone and inform him of his unanimous call by the members of this church that are present, be discharged. The motion receiving a second, was adopted. The Church then adjourned to meet at their next regular meeting to be held Wednesday night next before the first sabbath in November."

The sisters were called upon to collect money for several items, as shown in the minutes for October 2, 1871. "Bro. Graham moved that the thanks of the church be tendered to the committee of sisters who have so zealously assisted in the collection of the pastor's salary, and that they be requested to continue in the good work." The minutes continue, "After some very pertinent remarks from Bro. Griffith upon the duty of the servants of the church to whom such work properly belonged, the motion was adopted." The women still had no vote in church conference.

It was during Dr. Boone's pastorate that for the first time a young member of the church was ordained to the ministry.

"May 17, 1872. Met in conference. It was moved that this church appoint a Presbytery with a view to the examining and ordaining of Bro. Thomas J. Rooke to the Gospel Ministry. The motion being seconded was put to the church and unanimously adopted. It was proposed that the Presbytery consist of Rev. J. C. Furman, Rev. A. D. Phillips,

Rev. R. H. Griffith, and Rev. J. B. Boone. This proposition adopted.

"The Presbytery appointed to examine Bro. Thomas J. Rook being satisfied as to his call to the Gospel Ministry, proceeded on Sabbath night, May 19, 1872, to his ordination. Rev. James C. Furman preached the sermon. Rev. A. D. Phillips led in prayer. Rev. R. H. Griffith delivered the charge. Rev. J. B. Boone presented the Bible. Rev. Thomas J. Rook pronounced the benediction."

When Dr. Boone became the pastor, there was a flurry of activity and new life in the church springing from the innovations encouraged by the new pastor. There were committees appointed on lights, a financial system, and welcoming strangers. The church adopted a mission Sunday School which had been started by the teachers of the Charlotte Baptist Sunday School. A new financial plan was adopted, and an effort was made to correct the church roll.

At this period in its history the church received its first legacy. In the fall of the year, September, 1873, Deacon Vail in church conference produced the will of Mrs. Jane Spears, who had bequeathed her estate to the church. The amount was later learned to be $300, which was applied toward the building of a parsonage in 1875. This structure at the rear of the church building cost $1500. In her generosity to the church, Mrs. Spears had overlooked an item in her own behalf. Thirteen years later in 1886, Mr. J. C. Dowd called the attention of the church to this bequest, and reminded them that the remains of Mrs. Spears were interred near Hickory Grove, with nothing to mark her final resting place. A committee was appointed to raise funds to erect a suitable stone to mark her grave and to perpetuate her memory, and presumably this was done.

An important step in associational history was taken during this short pastorate. A new Baptist association was formed with the help of delegates from the Charlotte church. Earlier, in October of 1871, the Brown Creek Association — on request — had granted the Charlotte Baptist Church a letter of dismission. A committee of three was appointed by the church, July 31, 1872, to consider the matter of joining some more convenient association than the Brown Creek from which it had withdrawn. One month later the committee recommended that the church take no action on joining an association at present. The church met in special conference on June 18, 1873, to consider what action, if any, should be taken by the church in view of the proposed formation of a new association. The new body was to be composed of the churches located in the triangular section of the country of which Statesville, Salisbury, and Charlotte make the three angles. It was, after discussion, resolved that the church favored the formation of such an association, and that the pastor was authorized to appoint the delegates to represent the church at the proposed organization meeting on Friday before the fifth Lord's Day in July, 1873.

The story of the organization of the new association, known as South Yadkin Association, is told briefly in the minutes of the first session:

"October 17, 1873. In accordance with a resolution passed in meeting held at Cross Roads Church, October 6, 1873, delegates from churches in Iredell, Davie, Rowan, and Mecklenburg Counties met today at New Hope. Elder R. H. Griffith, Pastor at Charlotte, preached the introductory sermon from Acts 10:5, 6. Charlotte Church was represented by R. H. Griffith who was elected moderator of the new association. A mission board and a Sunday School board were appointed. The Charlotte Church joined the new association."

In the spring of 1873 a letter was received by the church from the Central Committee on the Board of Education of the North Carolina Baptist State Convention. It requested that Dr. Boone be released from his duties at the Charlotte church in order to act as the board's agent in assisting to raise a $100,000 endowment for Wake Forest College. The request was granted by the church, and the pastor resigned soon after.

At the time of Dr. Boone's resignation the church still owed him a part of his salary. In October in church conference it was announced that the balance past due to the former pastor was $222. In November the church was still struggling to take care of it.

"November 12, 1873. Church met in called conference. Rev. R. H. Griffith acting as Moderator. This being a special meeting on the matter of balance due on former pastor, Rev. J. B. Boone. Bro. Vail stated that other pledges had been made, and about One Hundred and Forty-two ($142) was yet unprovided for. Bro. S. P. Smith made remarks urging members to pay up the amount that they had subscribed, so as not to allow individual members to pay the debt. Bro. Vail made some feeling remarks urging the raising of the balance due, that the balance would be paid, but that it was a church debt. Bro. Griffith made some appropriate and happy suggestions as to punctuality in church business matters, and strongly and feelingly urged the adoption of such a line of policy, as would save trouble and delicacy of feeling. Being now without a pastor we should adopt systematic arrangements for the future. A motion was made and adopted requesting the church clerk to give all delinquents notice requesting all dues be paid between this and next regular conference. Conference adjourned. W. Boyd, Clk. pro tem. Rev. R. H. Griffith, Modr."

By the next April the debt had been paid and $728 had been raised to be applied to the next pastor's salary.

Dr. Boone for several years continued to make his home in Charlotte, where he is credited with having instituted in 1873 the first graded school in the state. The school, privately funded, replaced Charlotte's one-room school. The last work performed by Dr. Boone for the Baptists was as Manager of the Orphanage at Thomasville. Miss McLean described this fine educator and organizer as a man of great physical and moral courage, who was undaunted and undismayed no matter what happened, and who always carried through on his convictions when he felt that he was right.

After Dr. Boone's resignation, while the church was without a minister for over a year, the congregation was blessed with the preaching of excellent supply pastors, among whom was the well-known and respected Baptist leader, Dr. John A. Broadus. In September of 1874 a revival meeting provided the church's next pastor. An October entry to the church minutes provides a summary of the call of Dr. Theodore Whitfield to Charlotte:

"Supplemental Minutes. Entered Oct. 28, 1874. Owing to his absence, and lack of previous minutes, the clerk submits the following synopsis to be entered upon the records of the church. Rev. Theodore Whitfield, late of Meridian, Mississippi, accepted the invitation to visit this church previously given, and arrived on the first Sunday in September 1874, as did also Rev. Clarence M. Dixon, of Shelby, N. C. These brethren labored faithfully in the church for a fortnight, and their preaching was blessed with a gracious outpouring of the Holy Spirit. During and since that time 21 persons have been added to the church by baptism and six by letter.

"On the second Sunday in September, the church convened in special conference, and elected Rev. Theodore Whitfield as Pastor, pledging him a salary of Twelve Hundred dollars to be paid in monthly instalments. This call has been extended through the Deacons, the pastoral year to begin Sept. 1st, 1874, and Brother Whitfield has accepted and entered upon his duties."

During the last month of 1874 two items were brought before the church in conference. On the death of Bro. Wm. Gleason, the church extended its sympathy in the following manner:

"Whereas it hath pleased our Divine Master to remove our Brother, William Gleason, on the 7th of November, 1874, from the sufferings of this world to the rest which remaineth for all his saints, Resolved that this church sympathizes with the bereaved family and commends them to the prayers of all its members, and that a copy of the above preamble and resolution be sent to the family."

The other matter concerned an improvement to the church building.

"Resolved that this church tender its thanks to Dr. C. J. Fox for his liberality in the item of Gas furnished this church prior to September last. A committee of three were appointed to make the necessary arrangements in the Baptistry Dressing Rooms with a view to converting them into an Infant Class Room with stove and carpet, and folding doors in place of the present partition, without interfering with their continued use as Baptistry Rooms."

In February of the next year, 1875, another member departed from this life, and again the church underscored its Christian view of death in an appropriate resolution.

"Whereas in the Providence of our Heavenly Father our colaborer and Christian brother, Deacon J. B. Tolleson, has been called from the work of the Master among us, Resolved that while our hearts are bereaved by the great loss which we have sustained, we are rejoiced at the blessed assurance that he hath entered into the rest which remaineth for the people of God, and we shall ever cherish his memory as that of a faithful witness for Jesus. Resolved that we tender to his family our deepest sympathy in their afflictions."

Miscellaneous matters during this time ranged from the State Convention to the local Sunday School. The Charlotte Church entertained the Baptist State Convention for the third time. A Committee on Hospitality was appointed with nine members. Six delegates to the convention were selected, and a month before the meeting the treasurer was authorizd to pay certain expenses to be incurred in cleaning the church.

On the associational level, each year delegates were appointed to represent the church at the annual meeting of the South Yadkin Association. Among the delegates were the ministers who were members of the church, Rev. Whitfield, Rev. Griffith, Rev. Rooke, and Rev. Boone, along with laymen of the congregation.

Within the church was always the unity in diversity peculiar to Baptists. There was agreement in a supportive tribute to the Deacons on October 29, 1879, when it was resolved "that Brethren T. H. Vail, W. A. Hoffman, and J. C. Dowd, the Deacons of this church, deserve the confidence and cooperation of the entire membership; that they are hereby assured of our gratitude for their faithfulness in the past, and of our cordial support in the future; and that we desire hereby to encourage them to renewed zeal in the conduct of its spiritual and temporal business."

Diversity appeared in a Sunday School report.

"Bro. Hoffman, as Secretary of the Sunday School, made an informal report to the effect that there had arisen a difference of opinion in the school as to the best manner of choosing its officers, and in a Teachers' Meeting the subject had been referred to the church.

"Therefore, after some discussion pro and con, it was resolved that it is the sense of this church that the officers of the school should be elected as heretofore, to wit: by a majority vote of the whole school, each scholar, teacher, and officer being entitled to one vote; and the elections to be held at such times as the Teachers shall designate."

In 1879 the annual Treasurer's report was given as follows:

Church collection for twelve months	$64.88
Balance Poor Fund from last year	14.15
Poor Fund collected this year	13.75
Total	$92.78
Paid for Gas	$8.
For two loads wood	1.
For fees to Sexton	60.
Balance due Sexton for '77 and '78	27.45
Total	$96.45
Due to date for Gas	$14.

"On motion the amount to credit of Poor Fund was placed to credit of Incidental Fund, to be paid to Sexton, and the Treasurer instructed to endeavor to raise by subscription amount to pay off Gas Bill."

The ladies of the church never let go of the hope for a new church building. Mrs. Whitfield organized the Women's Aid and Benevolent Society, which name was later changed to the Ladies' Aid Society. The Ladies' Building Society prodded the entire congregation toward their goal of a new church. They made loans of the funds they had on hand to the men to complete the parsonage.

In November of 1876 the ladies sent a letter to be read at the church conference, urging immediate action toward raising funds for building a new house of worship. Obligingly the men in conference appointed a committee of six members to canvass the church and the community to secure subscriptions for building a new house of worship, naming six women to the committee. Four months later it was resolved in church conference "that the thanks of the church are due and hereby tendered to the Ladies' Building Society for their persevering efforts in raising funds for a new church building, and especially for the handsome entertainment lately given by them for the same object."

While the church was hopefully moving toward acquiring a more adequate place to worship, an internal matter disrupted the fellowship. Personal and business differences between two of the leading members, which they brought into the church, were becoming too difficult to lend themselves to solution within the membership. The impasse led to the only recorded instance when outside help was sought by the church to settle a difficulty within its membership.

It was agreed in church conference to ask five revered Baptist ministers from surrounding areas to arbitrate the altercations between the two men. Three of the invited preachers accepted the responsibility to act as an Advisory Council to help the church reach a conclusion in the matter. Rev. Thomas H. Pritchard, Rev. J. B. Taylor, and Rev. C. Durham spent two days with the church, listening to spokesmen on both sides of the controversy and questioning the two men involved in the case. After making an impartial and objective judgment, they presented it in writing to the church for acceptance or rejection. The membership in conference voted 15 to 12 to accept the decision of the ministers, with the clerk of the church recording in the minutes the names of those voting aye and no. Thus the matter was resolved.

Meanwhile, back at the planning table, progress was being made. On May 30, 1877, the church instructed the Deacons as Trustees to purchase on the best terms they could make the property known as the Harris lot, on the east side of Tryon, between Sixth and Seventh streets. On June 6 it was reported that the lot had been purchased "for the sum of $2125, $1000 of which they had paid in cash (the same having been raised principally through the efforts of the ladies of the church), and the balance was divided into three notes of $375 each, payable one, two, and three years respectively after date, with eight per cent interest, and secured by mortgage upon the premises. The registered Deed and receipts were handed in at the same time. Several of the brethren, including the Pastor, gave expression in timely remarks, to the thankfulness felt by the church at this mercy vouchsafed from the Lord."

At the same business session, "Sister Crawford sent in a request that the church establish a Missionary Sunday School in her part of the city. The church resolved to give the movement its approval, and Bro. J. B. Franklin by unanimous vote was appointed to take charge of it."

The next year when the first note became due on the Tryon Street property, "The Ladies Committee of Ways and Means to raise funds to pay note maturing on the 1st of June 1878, handed in $64.45 collected from Festival and otherwise. No member of similar committee of gentlemen was present to report. Funds from other sources for the same object were reported, making the total $114.80."

On July 3, Dr. W. H. Hoffman, on behalf of the Deacons, stated

"that the note for part of purchase money for the new church lot, maturing June 1st had been paid and cancelled, also that about $50 had been contributed toward the payment of the next succeeding note. It was further ascertained that the new proceeds of the late Greenville Excursion and Concert would amount to a little over $100 to be applied to the same object.

"The thanks of the church were voted to Mrs. Morgan and the ladies assisting her, for their zeal in projecting and carrying through to success this enterprise."

It was recorded in the Church Book that in October

"it was ordered that the Treasury pay the burial expenses of the late

Mrs. N. Crawford, who died in the fellowship of this church, and a collection be had on next Sunday morning for the Poor Fund. The Deacons as Trustees of the church were instructed to apply to the city authorities for a deed to the lot selected in the cemetery for this church and to have the same registered.

"Nov. 20, 1878. Committee of Deacons reported that they had obtained a Deed for the Lot in the cemetery granted by the city to the church and had had the same duly recorded."

The cemetery was Old Settlers Cemetery adjacent to the grounds of the First Presbyterian Church.

In the same conference "after considerable debate a resolution in the following form was adopted: That a Committee of Three be appointed to canvass the city of Charlotte to solicit contributions to aid in building a new church to cost not less than $10,000. That said Committee shall have authority to correspond with architects, and otherwise proceed to procure designs for the building, but not to bind this church to the acceptance of a plan, or for any expense thereby incurred, until approved by this church in conference. The Committee appointed are Brethren Hoffman, Walton, and Boyd."

The church was ready to pay the second note on the lot six months early. "January 15, 1879. Bro. Hoffman reported payment of second note given for purchase of new church lot at a discount of 5 percent (payment being in advance of maturity). This report was followed by remarks from the Pastor urging that efforts be made at once to cancel the remaining note, stating that $240 was all that was now lacking to complete all payments on the lot. Bro. B. F. Chalk offered to be one of twenty to pay $12 each. He was followed by similar offers from Bro. W. H. Huffman and the Pastor, who pledged two such payments. On motion a Committee consisting of Bros. Chalk and Pittman was appointed to call upon the the church, and endeavor to raise the necessary amount."

In April the last payment on the lot was made through the assistance of Dr. John H. McAden, and the church now held a clear title to the Tryon Street property. In May Bro. Graham reported that he had attended the Southern Baptist Convention in Atlanta, but that he was disappointed in getting any assistance toward building the new church. By the next September it was announced that about $4000 had been promised from all sources for the new church. Dr. Hoffman stated that he thought but little additional aid could be expected until the church should adopt a plan for the proposed new church edifice.

The plans presented by Architect A. L. West, of Richmond, Virginia, in March 1880 were revised after a month's consideration. In order to reduce the cost from $10,000 to $6,000, the proposed "pressed brick front was left off, and common brick substituted," and parts of the building were left off for the present, to be added later. A Building Committee was appointed "to take the whole matter in charge," and Mr. West was paid $115 for his plans and specifications. A contract was made for the wood and carpenter work for a little under $2200. A committee was named of one gentleman and four ladies to canvass the city and solicit money for the new church. After the foundation was laid, it was regarded as too small, and at the urgent request of Deacon W. J. F. Liddell, the length of the building was extended 17 feet. By summer, the Building Committee reported that the brick work in the building had been completed "up to the floor of the audience room, but was now at a standstill for want of funds."

With the work on the new building stopped, a "petition from the sisters to the male membership, suggesting certain improvements looking to the comeliness of our present audience room was read, and the matter was referred to the Deacons for early action." It was later reported that the pews had been painted.

In February of 1881 Dr. Whitfield offered his resignation to the church, but by an emotional and distressed response from the membership was persuaded to withdraw it. His reconsideration, however, was qualified by his intention to resign "unless there was greater progress." The church had during the past summer given him a leave of absence to take a trip to Europe, the second of two vacations granted him during his seven years' tenure, but the church was several hundred dollars in arrears on his salary and was reluctant to name a definite amount for the coming year. On December 31, 1881, Dr. Whitfield again tendered his resignation, with the church accepting it.

Dr. Whitfield had been an evangelist pastor, often holding protracted meetings in his own church. During one such meeting, held one year from April 22 to May 13, he was assisted by Rev. Jordan, the Volunteer State Evangelist, an effort which resulted in many baptisms in the church. The record says that "when Mr. Jordan bade the church adieu, he was followed by many prayers and tears." Mr. Jordan was "a soldier of the cross, who has preached in every section of North Carolina and has baptized in every river of the State." In most of his revivals, Dr. Whitfield preached alone.

According to Miss McLean, Dr. Whitfield was remembered as a man who loved to preach the love of God, and who stood high in the estimation and regard of the people. His accomplished wife was a help to him in all the work of the church. During his ministry about 100 persons were baptized and about the same number were received by letter. However, owing to changes of residence and other losses, at the close of his pastorate the church membership was only 150 persons. At his departure, the church borrowed money from the Mutual Building and Loan Association in order to pay the amount owed to him.

A resolution of the church on January 2, 1882, concerning his service included the following statements:

"We accept the resignation of Rev. Dr. Theodore Whitfield, now presented for the second time, and in the severence of the ties which have bound us so long and so closely together, take occasion to express the feelings we entertain for him as a faithful servant of the Most High. Much has been done by our devoted pastor and by his pious and accomplished family. We hold him in high esteem as an able theologian, eminent as well for his zeal as for his scholarly attainments; as a devout man of God, faithful as a preacher, earnest in his efforts to advance the cause of righteousness, upright in his walk and conversation, and gentle in manners, — in loveliness.

"Our prayers follow him and his that, sharing in the comfort which they have brought to others, their days may be long and full of blessings. Our thanks rise to God for the benefits we have received under his pastoral ministrations."

After the departure of Dr. Whitfield, Rev. Joseph E. Carter was called as pastor upon recommendation of the deacons in January, 1882, but declined. While the church was without a pastor for four months, the members assumed responsibility for its work. A committee of four was appointed on city missions, and a committee of five was appointed to seek out "such Baptists as are unconnected with us, who have come, and may hereafter come into this community."

In March of 1882 a church conference was called at the end of the morning worship service to elect a new pastor. The proceedings of the conference were unusual in that the Rules of Order were suspended to allow all members present to vote, a privilege usually exercised by men only. The result of the balloting was the unanimous calling of Rev. Oliver F. Gregory as pastor. The church pledged him an annual salary of not less than $800 and the use of the parsonage.

On April 2 Rev. and Mrs. Gregory were admitted to the fellowship of the church by letter from Cheraw, South Carolina. During the same month in a special conference, the long-time pastor and member of the church, Rev. R. H. Griffith, with his two daughters, Bettie and Maggie Griffith, were given letters of dismission to Greenville, South Carolina.

During the first church conference over which he presided in his new position, on April 12, Dr. Gregory proposed a set of resolutions which were adopted without objection, even though they departed drastically from the usual democratic procedures of a Baptist church. The idea of giving an executive committee authority for making decisions binding to the church was abandoned two years later, apparently not acceptable as a permanent plan to the congregation. Meanwhile, during its short life the method got the stalled church house built.

The new administrative program was so different from the usual Baptist way of doing things, both then and now, it is given here in full.

"Whereas it has been proven by past experience that frequent church conferences do not advance the harmony and usefulness of the church, and

"Whereas, it is best with a new pastor to have thorough reorganization of the working plans of the church

"Therefore, be it resolved:

I. That the Deacons and Clerk of the church with an equal number of male members, and the Pastor as chairman, be appointed an Executive Committee, to take charge of all the temporal and financial concerns of this church with full power to act, and that they submit a synopsis of all their doings to a full conference of the church to be held on the first Monday in July, October, January, and April, but shall have no power to incur any indebtedness without special authority from the church.

II. That the present Building Committee be dismissed and the Executive Committee instructed to proceed with the work of erecting the new House of Worship as rapidly as possible without incurring debt.

III. That the action of the church electing several treasurers be annulled and that the Executive Committee appoint one treasurer who shall receive, pay out, and account for all monies of the church in such a manner as the committee may require; and that the committee may appoint such of their number as may seem best to attend to the various objects to which we contribute.

IV. That we pledge our hearty support and cooperation to these brethren in their responsible and arduous work.

V. That the Executive Committee be instructed to meet at least once a month, at such a time and place as may be agreed upon among themselves.

VI. That we recognize in the Women's Missionary Society a great power for good and request them to act as a Committee on Missions and that they endeavor to secure systematic contributions for missions from every member of the church, and that the pastor be requested to aid them in this work.

VII. That the Ladies of the church be urged to unite themselves with the Ladies Aid Society in their laudable enterprise and undertaking.

VIII. That we recognize in "The Gleaners" a great power for good and urge all our young members to identify themselves with this society.

IX. That all previous resolutions regarding public collections in the church and Sunday School be annulled, and that the Executive Committee prepare such a schedule, as may seem to them for the best interest of the church, — This section is not to be construed as relating to any subscriptions hitherto made.

X. That the Executive Committee be requested to cooperate with the Superintendent in devising means to supply the needs of the school, and increasing its usefulness.

XI. That the Executive Committee be instructed to revise the Roll of the Church and present at each quarterly conference the names of those who are subject to discipline; provided that no charges shall ever be brought against a member in church conference until after every scriptural effort has been made to reclaim the wanderer and the offending party has been personally interviewed by the pastor, and at least one of the Committee, or corresponded with if he or she shall have left the city."

The pastor on April 16 added the names of seven men to those of the deacons to serve on the Executive Committee. The seven were J. M. Brewer, C. W. Eddins, E. K. P. Osborne, W. F. Williams,

W. F. J. Liddell, T. M. Pittman, and S. E. Todd. In July the name of Bro. M. Stauffer was substituted for that of J. M. Brewer. In October Bro. C. W. Eddins, having moved to Atlanta, was replaced by Bro. F. R. Durham.

The Executive Committee immediately began to revise the roll of the church, adding names which had been unintentionally omitted, and giving members who had moved from the city notice to join a church near their present abode. If there was no church near them, they could request that their names remain on the church roll provided that at least once a year they report to the pastor concerning their spiritual condition, and provided that they contribute to the support of the pastor, to the completion of the new church, and to the missionary enterprises of the denomination.

In June in a special conference, letters were granted to former pastor, Rev. Theo. Whitfield, Mrs. Whitfield, and Morehead Whitfield. In June also the pastor's son, O. F. Gregory, Jr., was received as a candidate for baptism upon his profession of faith.

In July the Executive Committee announced to the church in its regular quarterly report, that:

Bro. T. L. Vail had been appointed Church Treasurer.

Bro. W. H. Huffman had been appointed Sub-Treasurer on Pastor's Salary and Church Collections; Bro. T. M. Pittman, Sub-Treasurer on Church Expenses; and Bro. W. F. Williams, Sub-Treasurer on the Building Fund for the new church.

Collection boxes for the new church fund had been placed near the church doors.

An Envelope System for the collection of all contributions had been adopted for both the church and the Sunday School.

The Executive Committee also announced current progress on the new church building. The contractors of both the brick and wood work had declined to resume operations that summer, pleading previous engagements. Other persons equally satisfactory could be employed when funds were sufficient to justify it, under the well understood intention to pay as they go. Bro. T. L. Vail had been instructed to advertise the present church and lot (exclusive of the parsonage property) for sale at the cash price of $1500, the offer to be good until August 1.

Until this time, Miss Mclean reports, the church had not been able to buy hymnbooks, and it was the duty of the assistant superintendent of the Sunday School on each Friday night to stencil a hymn from the one hymnbook owned on a piece of muslin. On Sunday morning this was placed before the school, supported in a wooden framework designed and constructed by the assistant superintendent, so everyone could see. The Committee recommended the *Baptist Hymn Book* as the best and asked each member to purchase his own copy. In concluding its quarterly report, the Committee strongly urged the church to provide funds to resume work on the new church by August and plan to raise $2000 more by October. They added, "The foundation has stood the long exposure remarkably well, but we fear that another winter may prove just one too many."

In August the following resolution was introduced to the church and unanimously adopted: (1) To ask for a loan from the American Baptist Home Mission Society of New York City for such a sum of money as they may be willing to lend; (2) To offer the property on the corner of Brevard and Seventh Streets as security for the loan at a valuation of $4000; and (3) To insure the church and parsonage against fire and make the policy payable to the American Society for the amount of the loan.

By October the work had been resumed on the uptown Church, and the walls were ready to receive the roofing timbers. Along with the $1400 obtained from the American Baptist Home Mission Society, a liberal response to pledges already made and further canvassing were necessary, the Committee thought, to render the house habitable. In December the trustees of the church were authorized to sell the church and parsonage property on Brevard and Seventh, provided the price was not under $3500.

In May of 1883 the church in conference resolved to continue the Executive Committee for twelve months. At this time Rev. Gregory found it necessary to call the church's attention to the unpaid arrears in his salary. A committee was appointed to look into the matter and to canvass the members for contributions. The pastor's salary was set at $1000 a year instead of the $800 promised him, the 1882 arrears was paid, and most of the 1883 overdue amount was paid. It was reported that there were 107 members of the church who were not contributing to this object. The committee on the pastor's salary instructed the Executive Committee to try to receive a contribution from every member by monthly installments.

During this pastorate the matter of church discipline continued to be handled promptly. We read in the minutes book that on

"July 4, 1883, the church met in special conference, Brother B——— having been notified to appear before the church to say why fellowship should not be withdrawn from him for Profanity and other disorderly walk and conversation." The brother "returned word by Bro. C. S. Holton that he had no defense to make, and did not wish to be considered longer as a member. On motion fellowship was withdrawn.

"Sept. 4, 1883. Executive Committee recommended withdrawal of fellowship from Bro. J———, who had made no response to notice to show cause why this course should not be taken with him.

"Dec. 26, 1883. In regular conference, F———, B———, and B——— had fellowship withdrawn from them for disorderly walk. Mrs. G——— for same in connecting herself with a Christian church which has no Christian baptism."

In 1884 the church made the final moves to complete the new church building on Tryon Street. The Executive Committee was authorized in March to borrow not over $3000 to complete the new church, if necessary. The Deacons as Trustees of the church were authorized to mortgage the new building as security for the loan. On Sunday, March 22, 1884, the worship service was held in the basement of the new church. Sunday School was held at 9½ A. M. and Public Worship at 11 A. M. and 8 P. M. On the following Thursday, pledges which were begun on Sunday morning were reported to be $1500, to be paid in 60 days.

On a Sunday morning in May, after the worship service in the basement of the unfinished building, the congregation moved upstairs for the ordinance of baptism. Miss Florence Stokes, Miss Lilly Jarrett, and Mr. J. S. Simpson were the first to be immersed in the baptistry of the new church, as the church record says, "the first service held in the body of the new house of worship. The pastor made a short talk appropriate to the occasion."

On July 10 the Executive Committee reported the purchase of an organ for $410, of which $50 had been paid by the ladies, with the remainder to be paid in twelve monthly installments of $30 each. The Committee recommended that the Sunday night collections be applied to these payments.

The first Baptist church building on Tryon Street — finished, furnished, and occupied — was dedicated on Saturday evening, July 19, 1884. It was a glorious occasion for the congregation and for the past pastors of the church. The minutes book describes the event.

"July 19, 1884. This evening at 8:30 o'clock, the opening services in the main room of the new house of worship were held. Ministers present were Dr. Shaver, of Atlanta; Dr. J. C. Furman, of Greenville; Dr. Theodore Whitfield, of Goldsboro; Dr. R. H. Griffith, of Greenville; Rev. J. B. Boone, of Hendersonville; and Dr. O. F. Gregory, the pastor. Addresses were delivered by R. H. Griffith, J. B. Boone, and Theodore Whitfield, all the old pastors, but one, Rev. R. B. Jones, who has passed to his reward."

On the next morning, Sunday services were held with the sermon delivered by Dr. James C. Furman, who as a preacher boy had held that first Baptist revival in Charlotte in 1832, from which the first Baptist church in Charlotte had come into being. It was an historical sermon, relating the early efforts to establish a Baptist church in Charlotte, and telling of the chain of circumstances which called him to Charlotte in 1832, which seemed to have been directed by a higher hand. That the seeds he had planted then had brought forth an hundred fold was evidenced by the elegant edifice he was now helping to dedicate.

After the sermon, cash and pledges amounting to $763 were received to pay the balance of $618.36 still due on the work. At night the pastor made a report showing that $12,460.77 had been expended on the lot and building, of which the church and its societies had given $8,434.82; Baptists outside of Charlotte, $1,921.95; citizens of Charlotte, not Baptists, $704; borrowed on old church building, $1,400.

Under Dr. Whitfield's pastorate $4,917.44 had been collected in cash, besides pledges to be paid later, and the remainder had been collected under Dr. Gregory's pastorate. The pastor also enumerated the following special gifts: Mrs. J. L. Morehead, the memorial window; the Ladies' Aid Society, in addition to paying largely on the lot, the carpet and $50 on the organ; the Gleaners' Society, the church windows; Mrs. Murphy's class, the pulpit chairs, table, silver pitcher and goblet; Mrs. O. F. Gregory's class, the pulpit Bible and hymn book; the Violet Society, the collection baskets and organ screen; the Young People's Association, the granite steps; the baptistry was the gift of Prof. J. W. P. Jenks, of Middleton, Mass., in memory of his wife; and Mrs. Brokenborough, of Richmond, gave the book-marks.

After this report, a doctrinal sermon was preached by Dr. Lansing Burrows, of Augusta, Ga.

The following dedication hymn, written for the occasion by Dr. Lansing Burrows, inscribed to Mrs. O. F. Gregory, was sung:

> Arise, with loud acclaim,
>   The God of Mercy praise.
> All honor to the Name
>   To whom this house we raise;
> His grace began; His love completes;
> And now our song His favor greets.
>
> Thy works send out, O Lord,
>   The savor of Thy grace.
> As oft our feet have trod
>   The portals of this place.
> We've thought upon Thy conquering power,
> And waited long for this glad hour.
>
> 'Twas sovereign grace that made
>   Courageous those weak hands,
> That the foundations laid,
>   Where now this temple stands.
> Oh, may our faith like theirs be strong
> And conquer, though it wait as long.
>
> This house is incomplete,
>   With beauty glorified,
> If on Thy mercy seat
>   Thou comest not to abide.
> Accept our temple for Thine own,
> And make our grateful hearts Thy home.

During the following week a special conference was held to adopt resolutions of thanks to the pastor, to the visiting ministers who assisted in the opening exercises, and to the contributing friends. A specific resolution of thanks was passed for the organist, Miss Addie Williams, and for the choir for the special music performed at the dedication. The pastor, after his invigorating work, was offered a month's leave of absence.

Only three months after the dedication of the new church building, the Executive Committee was dismissed as being an unsatisfactory arrangement. In its place were established ten committees on which every male member of the church was asked to serve. The committees were on balance due the building fund, on condition of the building, on the poor, on music, on seating strangers, on the sale of the old property, on the Sunday School, on finances, on discipline and the revision of the church roll, and on missions.

Soon after Dr. Gregory resigned, preaching his farewell sermon on February 8. A few days later he left for his new field of work in New Orleans, and later he moved to the suburbs of Baltimore. During his pastorate there, the church he served was named the Gregory Memorial Church. For 39 years he was one of the honored secretaries of the Southern Baptist Convention. In Charlotte his greatest work was his part in building the Baptist church on Tryon Street.

Tryon Street, when the 1884 building was erected, was still unpaved, hard packed and serviceable in dry weather but muddy when it rained. The Square, which was two and one-half blocks south of the church, was graced on the southeast corner by the Central Hotel, called the finest between Richmond and Atlanta. On the opposite corner was the Jordan Drug Store, where the Independence Building has stood since 1908. The City Hall was on the northeast corner of Tryon and Fifth Streets, described as a substantial brick building with elaborate brownstone trimmings and with an impressive cupola. The city had a population of 8000. Horsedrawn buses had become the mode of public transportation, and Fourth Ward was becoming the fashionable place to live.

Mr. J. Howerton Alexander, who presently attends First Baptist Church, remembers seeing the 1884 building as a boy when he came from his home in Cornelius to visit Charlotte. He recalls riding in a relative's horse-drawn carriage along Tryon Street, which was planked from the Square as far north as Sixth Street. He remembers the fine homes on either side of Tryon, built on banks rising higher than the street, some of them elegant white structures with black iron fences. There in the midst of them stood the red brick church with its granite steps and white steeple. Future history would attest that it was a wise step when the Baptists moved to the center of town.

Chapter 5 | The First Baptist Church of Charlotte, 1885–1917

With a new church building on Tryon Street, the pastorate of A. G. McManaway was an encouraging period of seven years, during which the Charlotte Baptist Church passed from a struggling congregation to a stable one. The membership of the church increased, its organization was strengthened, and the economic recovery of the city from Reconstruction perils was reflected in the growth of the church. When Rev. McManaway left the pastorate after seven years, he rightfully called his work finished.

Rev. McManaway was called by the Charlotte congregation from the Baptist church in Louisburg, North Carolina, on April 15, 1885. In May he preached for the church. The minutes of the church read, "May 3, 1885. Rev. A. G. McManaway filled the pulpit morning and evening and in the afternoon had an informal conference with church in which he stated that he would not be able to move to Charlotte before fall even if he accepted the call. Church announced that it expected to pay salary of $1200 and house." The new pastor assumed his duties on October 25, 1885.

On Sunday, November 8, he began a revival meeting, doing the preaching himself, which lasted until November 17. "Tuesday night, Nov. 17th. Closed a protracted meeting conducted by our pastor Rev. A. G. McManaway during which time 24 persons were received for baptism and 4 by letter. Making a total of 28."

Early in his pastorate, the familiar story of financial struggle was written in the minutes of June 22, 1886, with the treasurer's reporting the church to be about $500 in debt. Then the old Brevard Street property was sold for $2500, and the proceeds were applied to paying off all remaining debts of the church. At the end of the

year in his Annual Report, the Treasurer, Mr. T. L. Vail, closed
with the following remarks:

"I congratulate the church on the fact that we can now have the
pleasure of worshipping in a building which we know is ours for the
Lord, and without fear of annoyance from the presentation of any
bills on account of our undertaking to build a house for His name,
which has caused many of us much anxiety and much sacrifice, and
the completion of which reflects much credit on His people. I would
do violence to my feelings and withhold that which is meet and proper
were I not in this connection to make some allusion to some of the
noble brethren (omitting names) who have so generously come forward
during the year and contributed of their means at a time when the
treasury was empty, — claims being presented and nothing to pay with.
They are entitled to the thanks of the church as well as the lasting remembrance of the membership. It is also very gratifying to add that
while many of the male membership have been deriving ways and
means for the liquidation of our indebtedness and pushing forward
the cause we profess to love, the best part of our membership (to wit,
our good Sisters) have by their godly example and exhibition of their
strong faith in the great Head of the Church, encouraged many of us
and bade us go forward. To the female membership of this church is
largely due the credit for what has been accomplished in the building
of this house and freeing it from debt. May we all live long and har-
moniously together and esteem it a privilege to work for the Master."

It was now a stronger church which continued in its cooperation
with fellow Baptist churches in associational enterprises, giving
both leadership and money. When the South Yadkin Association
met at New Hope Church in September 1886, the Charlotte Church
requested a letter of dismission to join the Mecklenburg-Cabarrus
Association, which was to be organized the following month.

The first session of the Mecklenburg-Cabarrus Baptist Association was held at the Coldwater Church, Cabarrus County, October
14, 1886. Charlotte Baptist Church, represented by the pastor, Rev.
McManaway, was received into the association. Later, the Cabarrus
Baptist Association was organized in 1935, and the Charlotte
Church has remained in the Mecklenburg Baptist Association and
has shared in all the activities of the association.

It was in February, 1887, that Miss Eva Liddell organized in the
Charlotte Church the Christian Endeavor Society, which was not

only the first in the city but the first in the state. The records say that the first meeting was led by T. S. Franklin and the subject, "Influence," was discussed. Some time before 1903, the Christian Endeavor Society became the Baptist Young People's Union. In that year *The Charlotte News* announced that John H. Weathers would deliver his famous chalk talk to the B. Y. P. U. Meeting to be held on Monday night.

In 1888 the church established its next city mission, the Trade Street Mission.

"June 20th, 1888. Bro. McManaway, our pastor, made the following statement. For sometime he and the board of deacons have been considering the advisability of building another Baptist church, that this has been brought to their attention on account of the cotton factories which are now being erected in our midst which will necessarily cause an influx of a class of people which can best be reached by carrying the gospel to their doors, and in addition to this, the duty we owe to our Savior to work in His vineyard, to use our every effort to give everyone an opportunity of hearing the glad tidings, and again, that we as Baptists should not be behind any denomination in the noble work of spreading the gospel. Bro. McManaway further stated that where would be the best place to establish a new church had been looked into thoroughly and that they, the board of deacons and himself, had decided that the best location would be in Ward 3 on the corner of Trade and Cedar Streets. This lot he further stated was owned by Mrs. Osborne and that she had offered to sell it to the church for $500."

The lot was purchased, and largely through the efforts of Mr. W. J. F. Liddell, a building costing $1500 was erected. The payments were arranged for through the Building and Loan Association, Mr. Liddell being one of sixteen men who agreed to carry the shares at 50 cents a week. (If the amount of the shares seems odd to the reader, take note this was the period when manufacturing plants were being built in Charlotte with stock shares purchased for 25 cents per week.) A committee of ladies of the church raised the necessary $500 to buy the lot for the mission. On November 5, 1890, thirty-eight members were dismissed to organize the church. The Trade Street mission was named by Mrs. Liddell, "Olivet," and the mother church then became known as the Tryon Street Church. The mission church functioned for about 15 years, then was sold to the Presbyterians, who used it as the West Avenue Presbyterian Church.

In those days church discipline was still a strong factor of church life.

"June 22, 1886. Bro. F————, through our pastor, asked that his name be dropped from the roll of the church, as he had not been living the life of a Christian for several weeks past. After some discussion, on motion a committee of two was appointed to confer with Bro. F————.

"Aug. 31st. The committee appointed to confer with Bro. F———— stated that he was now attending church regularly and appeared to be satisfied."

The male members were cited if they missed three successive business meetings; on one occasion a brother admitted he had no excuse, and for his frankness was excused for having no excuse.

One matter of discipline concerned Charlotte's Opera House, which had been built about 1874 on the corner of South Tryon and Fourth Streets, an elegant structure whose interior boasted 900 crimson plush seats.

"Feby 29th, 1888. The board of deacons presented the following through Bro. E. K. P. Osborne, which was unanimously adopted: Whereas we believe that many of the operas and plays presented in our city are light, frivolous and demoralizing in their tendencies, and whereas we believe the modern dance as usually conducted at balls, sociables and other places of amusements to be detrimental to the cause of Christ and that His followers ought not to participate in it, Therefore it is Resolved that the members of this church be and they are hereby requested and urged not to encourage such plays or operas by their presence, nor impair their usefulness and impede the Master's cause by participating in such dance. On motion the pastor was instructed to read the preceding adoption and the Church Covenant Sunday morning next."

When W. J. F. Liddell, deacon of the church, a prominent citizen of Charlotte, and owner of the Liddell Foundry on North Pine Street, died, four pages in the minutes book were devoted to a eulogy to this fine Christian. The following brief excerpts are taken from the tribute.

"This devout deciple of Jesus Christ. . . . identified himself with our people in every interest: religious, social, and commercial. . . . Greater personal impressions of character have been made by few men upon their community. . . . Born to leadership in the affairs of the church, his example was an inspiration to action. It is with gratitude to God we chronicle his child like trust as a sinner in the merit and sufficiency of Jesus Christ his Savior. . . . The last noble work of Bro. Liddell was the erection of the beautiful chapel on the corner of Trade and Cedar Sts. now just completed, and built through Bro. L.'s earnest and never tiring efforts. One of the most impressive and beautiful memorial services was held in the Baptist church in honor of Bro. Liddell. The church was beautifully draped in mourning, and the services conducted by Rev. F. D. Swindell of the Methodist church, Rev. W. R. Atkinson, Pres't Charlotte Female Institute, and Rev. A. G. McManaway the pastor. May the smiles of heaven be upon his bereaved family."

Among other events of Dr. McManaway's pastorate was the decision to elect deacons on a staggered basis, with deacons elected on the first ballot to serve for three years, those elected on the second ballot to serve for two years, and those elected on the third ballot to serve one year, with vacancies being filled each year thereafter. Extensive repairs were completed on the church building, while the congregation met in the hall of the Y. M. C. A. There was a successful revival in 1892, again adding many members to the church.

Rev. McManaway greatly surprised the church when he submitted his resignation on August 7, 1892, which the members refused to accept. During the ensuing week the clerk read the following letter from the pastor:

Dear Brethren and Sisters:
The resignation now pending is final. My work among you is finished. My farewell sermon has been preached. If I have omitted any work or teaching, exhortation, warning or reproof, it would not be worthwhile to supply it now. If none were omitted I could not repeat any of them with greater emphasis than I have used before, hence I have but to ask you now that you remember the words that I spoke unto you while I was yet with you.

I trust it will be your good pleasure to publish no complimentary resolutions with reference to my work among you. If that work has been of the right sort, it will speak for itself through the years that are to come. If it has not been of the right sort, complimentary resolutions cannot bolster it up, so I ask that you kindly leave it to stand on its own merits. Let me add, however, that I am not insensible to the kind expressions that have been used with reference to my resignation. From minister and layman, Jew and Gentile, saint and sinner, have come words that have touched my heart to the deepest core. Emotions too deep for utterance except by tears have more than once been stirred within me.

I bespeak for my successor the same cooperation from you and the same degree of recognition and kindness from the people generally that have been so freely accorded me.

And now farewell.

A. G. McManaway

On his departure from Charlotte, Rev. McManaway moved to First Baptist Church, Little Rock, Arkansas.

The record in the minutes book of the Charlotte Baptist Church, beginning on September 8, 1856, and extending to the last entry on October 29, 1890, ends during the pastorate of Rev. McManaway. For thirty years thereafter the records of the church are scant. Thanks be to God for the old Church Book, written and preserved for its members, whereby they may more fully understand the rich heritage that is theirs. The worn and priceless volume is presently kept in the church library.

The next pastor was Dr. Thomas Henderson Pritchard, who was first called to the church in 1885, a call which he declined. He was born in 1832, the year when the church was born, the son of James F. Pritchard, who was a charter member of the Beulah Baptist Church. Dr. Pritchard was the grandson of John Dinkins, the first Baptist in Mecklenburg County. As a boy, Thomas Pritchard attended Sunday School at the First Presbyterian Church, under whose trees he memorized the Westminster Shorter Catechism. This was during the time when the Beulah Baptist Church was dormant. He worked his way through Wake Forest College, graduating in 1854 as valedictorian of his class. In the early 1880's he was president of Wake Forest College and twice was the associate editor of the "Biblical Recorder," the state Baptist paper. It was said of Dr. Pritchard that he held more responsible positions and had been more honored by his brethren, had dedicated more churches and preached more ordination sermons than any minister in North Carolina. When Dr. Pritchard came to Charlotte in 1893, in a sense he was coming home. He had assisted R. B. Jones in reorganizing the Beulah Church and had served on the Advisory Council for the church. When he became pastor of the Charlotte Baptist Church, both he and the church were 61 years old. The work of the church was greatly strengthened by his short pastorate of a little more than three years.

Dr. Pritchard possessed the characteristics of a great minister of the gospel. He was a brilliant scholar, having read theology as a young man with Dr. John A. Broadus of Charlottesville, Virginia. Pulpits filled by him were the Baptist church in Fredericksburg, Virginia; the Franklin Square Church in Baltimore during the Civil War, where he was arrested and banished to the South for being a rebel; the First Church in Raleigh, N. C.; the First Church in Petersburg, Virginia; the Broadway Baptist Church, Louisville, Kentucky; and the First Church in Wilmington, N. C. He was an able administrator and a fervent evangelist. Also the warm-hearted pastor, he was called "Bre'r Rabbit" by little children, who loved to hear him tell Uncle Remus stories. He had a keen sense and a rich fund of humor, and as a platform speaker he was at his best.

During the first year of his pastorate, a Sunday School room was built at a cost of $2500, which was designed to seat 200 and included a pastor's study. At the same time the baptistry was moved and rebuilt.

Dr. Pritchard teamed with Dr. L. R. Pruette, who had been appointed city missionary, in evangelistic efforts and in the missions work of the city. Dr. Pruette was pastor at Olivet when the two pitched a tent on North Caldwell Street and preached alternately each night for four weeks in September, 1895. There were about 100 conversions, and a mission Sunday school was organized with workers going from the Tryon Church. The school first met in a small cottage on Thirteenth Street and later grew into the Twelfth Street Baptist Church, with twelve of the 18 charter members coming from the Tryon Street Church. In 1904 this church moved, becoming the Ninth Street Baptist Church, and in 1949 it again moved to Mecklenburg Avenue to become the Midwood Baptist Church.

Dr. Pritchard and Dr. Pruette organized a Sunday school under a tent near the Atherton Mill on October 27, 1895, after holding a month-long revival. It was moved to the Atherton Lyceum and was called the Atherton Sunday School. On September 9, 1900, it was moved again to Long Hall and named the Dilworth Sunday School. Forty-six people with letters from Tryon Street, Twelfth Street, and Olivet churches organized this mission into Pritchard Memorial Baptist Church on November 10, 1901. This was five years after Dr. Pritchard's death.

In 1894 the church was again host to the Baptist State Convention, and the Christian Endeavor Society invited all the Young People's Societies to meet in a convention on the preceding day. As a part of the preparation for the Convention, the ladies bought a new carpet at a cost of $350. It was a memorable meeting, with such speakers as Dr. R. H. Graves, the veteran missionary from China.

A feature of the Sunday School work of the Tryon Street Church in the nineties was the presence of several Chinese as pupils. Their teachers endeavored to teach them to speak and read English and, as they came to know the language, to inculcate as much of Christian truth as possible. As a result, according to Miss McLean, several of them gave up their idol worship and acknowledged Christ as their Savior. One of them went from Charlotte to New York and later wrote his teacher that he had joined one of the churches there and was preparing himself to go back to China as a missionary.

Dr. Pritchard passed away in May, 1896, at the home of his son in New York, where he had gone for medical treatment. His body was brought back to Charlotte to be buried in the city of his birth. The clergy of the city and the Knights of Honor attended his funeral in a body, as honor, love, and esteem from many sources were shown the pastor. Dr. Pruette, his longtime friend and fellow worker, made the following entry in his diary following the funeral:

"May 21, 1896 — The funeral exercise of Dr. Pritchard was conducted in Tryon Street Church as follows: Music, Invocation by Rev. L. R. Pruette, Hymn announced by Rev. Huffman. Prayer by Rev. H. L. Atkins. Hymn, Asleep in Jesus. 5000 or more attended the exercises." Dr. Pritchard was buried in Elmwood Cemetery. A memorial plaque was placed in the foyer of the church auditorium by the Young People's Mission Band. It read:

"Rev. Thos. H. Pritchard, D.D.
Pastor of this church from
January 1, 1893
To the close of his life
May 23, 1896
'A prince in Israel has fallen'
'For he was a good man and full
of the Holy Ghost and of faith'
Erected by
the Young People's Mission Band."

The turn-of-the-century pastor for the Tryon Street Church was introduced to Charlotte by a revival meeting. In the summer of 1895, Dr. A. C. Barron and Dr. H. M. Wharton of Baltimore held the meeting which lasted for several weeks. It was held under the auspices of the Baptist churches with other denominations co-operating, and the services were held in the large auditorium which stood on West Sixth Street behind the Tryon Street Methodist Church (now the First Methodist Church). The building accommodated several thousand people and was filled at every service. By the end of that meeting it was said that all Charlotte had come to love Dr. Barron. It was natural, therefore, that the First Church should ask him to succeed Dr. Pritchard.

The church records for the period of Dr. Barron's pastorate are not available, but *The Charlotte News* and *The Charlotte Observer* supply information about the man and his work.

"Dr. Barron was born near Columbus, Georgia, May 31, 1844. His father died when he was eighteen months old. At nine years of age he was forced to make his own living, working with a newspaper. At the age of fifteen he was supporting himself and mother, and worked his way through college by setting type and studying at night. He graduated at Howard College in Alabama. He joined the Confederate Army, but was discharged because of ill health and again entered the newspaper business, editing a daily paper at Atlanta, Georgia. During the war, he read law under Judge Cleaton of Alabama for a short while, but changed his mind, and at the age of 19 began to study for the ministry.

"His first charge was Adams Street Baptist Church, Montgomery Alabama, 1870. He preached at Tuskegee, Alabama, two years and then at Lexington, Va., where he married Miss Addie V. Mason in 1874. He was called to the Baptist Church at Culpepper, Va., in 1875, and remained there until 1882, when he went to Berryhill, Va. In 1884 he took charge of Fulton Avenue Baptist Church, Baltimore, Md., where he did what he considered his life's best work, taking charge of a church with 40 members; in ten years his labor resulted in the building of a great church. While pastor of that church he was also the editor of the *Baltimore Baptist*. With Rev. H. M. Wharton, 1894, he began evangelistic work. For two years he met with remarkable success." (*Charlotte Observer*, August 20, 1905).

The newspapers also reported such activities of the church as participation in a city-wide religious census, the organization of Baraca and Philathea classes, the reaching of an attendance of 385 in Sunday School, the operation of Olivet Sunday School, the entertainment of the Baptist State Convention in 1903, and Sunday School excursions to Asheville for profit and pleasure. "Baby Day" was observed first on July 17, 1904. Dr. Barron led the church to employ Miss Carrie Booker of Mt. Airy as city missionary to work both at the church and at Olivet mission. The Sunday School was enlarged, and a parsonage was built at 506 North Tryon Street. The parsonage was on the east side of Tryon just beyond Eighth Street. Its title was held in the names of C. A. Duckworth, J. A. Yarborough, and A. L. Byrd as Trustees for First Baptist Church. Later it was sold to Dr. Hoffman, a dentist of the city, for $20,000, which was used to build a new Sunday School building.

A delightful reminiscence is taken from the scrapbook of Clyde A. Duckworth, longtime member and worker in the church. Mr. Duckworth came to Charlotte as a young attorney when the city had a population of 18,000. He recalls, "When I came to Charlotte to live in the early 1900's, I joined First Baptist Church. I was baptized in the old red brick church that stood on the site of our present location. Dr. A. C. Barron was the pastor and he baptized me in the old baptistry that was a rather crude affair and was located under the pulpit. Dr. Barron was a saintly man and muchly beloved by the people of Charlotte."

The humanitarian nature of Dr. Barron is shown by his reaction to a news story of that time. Miss McLean relates that a little four-year-old girl was burned to death while her mother was away from home earning a living. It was from this incident that Dr. Barron, perhaps remembering his own difficult childhood, organized the

Charlotte Day Nursery Association to care for little children in the absence of their mothers while the latter earned daily bread.

Dr. Barron's first sermon in Charlotte was "The Scarlet Line in the Window," a sermon repeated several times by request and one he loved to preach, extolling the theme of which he never tired, the redemption that comes through the blood of Christ.

In June, 1905, Dr. Barron went to London to attend the International Baptist Congress, and afterwards gratified a life-long desire to see Europe. On the last Sunday in July he preached in one of the three Baptist churches in Paris, with the aid of an interpreter, before his voyage home. On the steamer he preached his last sermon. A large number confessed Christ, among them the captain of the ship. On his way home, he stopped at the home of his daughter in Somerset, Virginia, joining his family there. On the way to the station to return to Charlotte, he suffered a stroke of paralysis, from which he never recovered. He died August 19, and his body was brought to Charlotte where the funeral was conducted by the pastor of Pritchard Memorial Church and by Rev. R. L. Pruette. Dr. Barron was buried in Elmwood Cemetery near Dr. Pritchard.

The Charlotte Observer paid the following tribute:

"Dr. Barron was full of the milk of human kindness. He was temperate, generous, tolerant, valiant, honest and faithful. He loved his fellow-man and had a way about him that attracted all sorts of men to him. His heart went out to the weak man. Dr. Barron was a learned man, an able preacher, an eloquent speaker, an earnest Christian worker and a noble character. Saintly men loved him for his goodness and sinners for his kindness and liberality."

Once more the Young People's Mission Band with the help of the Baraca Class erected a memorial plaque in the foyer of the church auditorium, inscribed as follows:

"In Loving Memory of
Rev. Alonzo Church Barron, D.D.
'A preacher of righteousness'
May 3, 1844 — August 19, 1905
Pastor of this church 1896 — 1905
'For I determined to know nothing
among you save Jesus Christ and
Him crucified.' "

To the next pastor, the youngest ever called to the First Baptist Church, was given the task of leading the people to build the remarkable edifice which still stands on North Tryon Street. Rev. H. H. Hulten, a graduate of William Jewell College, who was pastor of First Baptist Church, Kansas City, Missouri, was called as pastor on April 15, 1906, at the age of 24 years. Dr. Hulten was an eloquent speaker, and immediately his preaching attracted overflow congregations.

The Sunday School room was again enlarged at a cost of $5000, the addition increasing the seating capacity from 500 to 1000. Its opening on November 17–18, 1906, was celebrated by a Chautauqua lasting for two days. This gathering brought to Charlotte some of the best known Sunday School workers in the country. On February 11, 1907, the city newspapers reported: "Yesterday at the First Baptist Sunday School 875 men, women and children were present. So far as can be learned that is the largest attendance ever accounted for at a local Sunday School."

As 1906 drew to a close, members of the church were discussing the need for a new church building. The congregation had grown so much that a larger structure seemed an absolute necessity. As evidence of this, the revival meeting of the Tryon Baptist Church in the fall was held in the Methodist Church because the Baptist auditorium was too small for the congregation. The plans for a new church were reported in *The Charlotte Observer*. "January 14, 1907, the church unanimously and enthusiastically adopted a recommendation of the deacons that a new church building be erected. J. A. Durham was elected chairman of the building committee. Others named to serve were T. S. Franklin, W. C. Dowd, R. H. Jordan, Willis Brown, H. G. Harper, and H. H. Hulten."

James M. McMichael was the architect for the new structure, and Mr. J. A. Gardner the contractor, both members of the First Baptist Church. Mrs. John Earnhardt, the daughter of the architect and presently a member of First Church, provided much information about her father. James Mackson McMichael, Sr., was born on December 14, 1870, in Harrisburg, Pennsylvania, and came as a young man to Charlotte in 1901. During his 50-year-long career as architect of public buildings, he designed 963 churches, schools, and colleges, no two of them alike. Among them were the First Baptist Church of Charlotte, the First ARP Church, the Bible Presbyterian Church, Myers Park Presbyterian Church, and the Public Library. Throughout the country there was marked improvement in church architecture due to his work and influence. He was invited to attend a Conference on Home Building and Home Ownership in Washington, D. C., by President Hoover in 1927. In spite of his acclaim, his daughter asserts that he was very modest and disliked publicity. Above all he loved his family.

A *Charlotte News* staff writer eulogized him at his death, writing about the sources of his inspiration. McMichael's original architectural concepts came to him from nature. He loved to walk in the woods, which he regarded also as a church glorifying the Almighty. The lordly trees were spires pointing to Heaven. The sky was a magnificent blue dome. The sunset clouds were designs for windows and the wind-blown flowers were decorations. Color schemes were abundant to his practiced eye in the trees and hills in all seasons. From these came the impressions which in long, silent hours he fitted to the architectural forms which mankind through the ages has created and preserved.

Clyde A. Duckworth in his scrapbook recalled helping to build the church. "It was the spring of 1906 that we members of First Baptist Church under the leadership of Dr. Herman Hulton (aged twenty-four when he came to us), decided that we should have a new church. Plans were inaugurated for a new $50,000 auditorium to seat more than 1000. We had a plan of selling members bricks to go into the building at one dollar per brick. I was anxious to have 300 bricks and paid for them by the month. How happy I was when I finished paying for my bricks and saw them go into the walls of the building. I love that dear old church. As I pass my church today, I often wonder which bricks are mine. Even though they look alike, it thrills me to know that somewhere there are my 300 bricks.

"The church building was designed by one of our loyal members, J. M. McMichael, a past master in church designing. He put his whole soul in designing his own church. Our beautiful pipe organ in the church was, at the time that it was installed, one of the finest and most beautiful in the Southland. This is the story of our pipe organ.

"Andrew Carnegie had made it possible for the city of Charlotte to build a fine library. It was built and opened about 1903. It was located next door to the old First Baptist Church. Just a driveway separated the two buildings. When Mr. Carnegie learned that we were going to build a new church next door to his library, he was anxious for our architecture to be compatible. He agreed to give $5000 on the purchase of an organ if we designed our church with that style architecture. It is said that when the church was completed, Mr. Carnegie was so delighted that he paid the full purchase price of the organ.

"The beautiful painting, 'The Good Shepherd,' was painted by Olsen, an artist who came here from New York City for that purpose. I dropped in often and watched while he was painting it. In later years I learned that Mr. Olsen was spending the evening years of his life in North Carolina at the Masonic and Eastern Star Home in Greensboro, and that he had a great yearning to see once again before he died what he considered to be his masterpiece, 'The Good Shepherd.' I was trying to arrange this with my daughter when he died. What a tragedy that we put off until tomorrow the good deeds that we should do today."

One of the bricks of the building bears the name of the architect, carved and misspelled by the workmen. Mrs. Earnhardt says, "If that building is ever razed, I want that brick."

The beautiful church, with its big Byzantine domes and arched stained-glass windows, its slanted floor and perfect acoustics, was dedicated on May 2, 1909, 25 years almost to the day since the first service was held in the auditorium of the old red brick church. The vast congregation overflowed the auditorium, and many were turned away. The dedication sermon was preached by Dr. E. Y. Mullins, president of the Southern Baptist Theological Seminary. It was said to be a masterly sermon whose subject was "Our Heritage." The text was Psalm 16:6, "The lines are fallen unto me in pleasant places; yea, I have a goodly heritage." The sermon presented the fundamental beliefs of Baptists, their heritage of providential guidance, their heritage of suffering, their trust in the competency of the individual soul in religion, under God. A musical program was rendered under the direction of Mrs. Alexander Stephens, using the new Mohler organ. Rev. D. M. Austin delivered the invocation, Rev. L. S. Conrad the morning prayer, and at the close of the sermon the dedication prayer was offered by the pastor, Dr. Hulten.

The church with a membership of 500 had built a sanctuary which would seat 1200 and which, including equipment, had cost over $50,000. It was one of the first in the nation to have the large central dome. The architect's son, David McMichael, also an architect who worked with his father during the last five years of the older McMichael's life until his death in 1942, has said that for guidance James McMichael studied drawings of the Hagia Sophia Cathedral of Constantinople, the most famous in the world in the Byzantine style.

Surrounding the sanctuary are 18 memorial stained-glass windows, whose panes were made by a Paterson, New Jersey company, then leaded together and installed by local workmen. The windows were donated by families and individuals to memorialize their loved ones. The windows were dedicated:

To James M. Smyly 1860–1903
by Sarah T. Smyly

•

To Joseph F. Mosteller
by Mr. and Mrs. A. F. Mosteller

•

In Memory of our Grandmother,
Cornelia Sigman 1845–1922
by Lucille Little and Mildred Sheets

•

Erected by 3-B Baraca Class
Which she taught for 10 years
to Eloise Dowd

•

To Rebecca C. Crimson 1837–1910

•

To Our Mother
(no other name)

•

To Helen M. Price 1856–1921

•

To Our Mother
(no name or date)

·

By C. W. Wise and Mrs. A. E. Walton

·

To Mrs. Lucy Dunbar Black
1844–1908

·

By his wife and children
(name cannot be read)

·

To James William Brown 1852–1921

·

Virginia Katherine Smith
by Father and Mother
Mr. and Mrs. Richard W. Smith

·

In Appreciation of
Bettie Harriet Yarbrough
Erected by
Mr. and Mrs. J. A. Yarbrough

Over the balcony of the church auditorium, the large window on the Seventh Street side on which the Ascension of Christ is pictured, was inscribed:

Jane Christian Boyd
1825–1903
"This woman was full of Good
Works and Almsdeeds"

The window was given by Mr. W. S. Forbes of Richmond in memory of his mother, a faithful member of the church in its Brevard Street days.

The large window on the Sixth Street side, showing Jesus and the Children, was inscribed:

Walter James Forbes Liddell
1825–1888
This memorial was given by his son, Mr. Vinton Liddell.

The building was occupied on May 2, 1909, just 18 days before

President William Howard Taft visited the city for the annual celebration of the signing of the Mecklenburg Declaration of Independence. Tryon Street and Trade Street were bedecked with banners and flags, all to be inundated along with Pres. Taft and other dignitaries in what was described as a torrential rain.

Three years later Dr. Hulten resigned in September, 1912, to become the pastor of the First Baptist Church in Oklahoma City. His pastorate was followed by that of Dr. W. W. Vines, who came from St. Joseph, Missouri, on the third call from the Charlotte church.

Dr. Vines began his work on the first Sunday of June, 1913. He was a Tennessean, born at Jonesborough in 1867. Educated at the University of Chicago and the Southern Baptist Theological Seminary, he held pastorates in Johnson City, Tennessee; Asheville, North Carolina; Norfolk, Virginia; St. Joseph, Missouri; and Greenwood, South Carolina.

Dr. Vines' appearance in the pulpit is remembered by one of the members as tall, slender, good-looking, distinguished, and dignified. His sermons were enriched by quotations from the secular classics, Scripture references, and historical illustrations. His preaching emphasis was evangelistic.

There were several revival campaigns of note during the four years of Dr. Vines' pastorate. In the fall of 1913 he conducted his own meeting, also in the spring of 1914 with the help of Dr. and Mrs. J. H. Dew of Liberty, Missouri. He served as chairman of the executive committee for a city-wide revival in 1915, which lasted for five weeks beginning in April. Most of the churches of the city cooperated, inviting Dr. J. Wilbur Chapman and Mr. Charles M. Alexander to conduct the services. An auditorium seating about 6000 people was erected on East Avenue (later called East Trade Street) and was filled at almost every service. Hundreds came from the surrounding towns and country. There were 1000 who professed conversion, and 200 of these joined First Baptist.

The increase in membership led to the hiring of Miss Susan Anderson of Atlanta as assistant to Dr. Vines. She was a graduate of the Training School in Louisville, Kentucky, and endeared herself to the people in Charlotte. Later she served as a beloved missionary to Nigeria.

The final revival of Dr. Vines' tenure was sponsored in 1916 by the Evangelistic Force of the Southern Baptist Home Mission Board, a city-wide campaign of two weeks for all the Baptist churches of Charlotte. The meeting resulted in 75 new members for First Baptist and 400 for the city at large. During the years prior to this time, the church had assisted the organizations of four more Baptist churches: Chadwick Baptist Church in 1903, North Charlotte Baptist Church in 1908, Allen Street, and Thrift.

Dr. Vines, described by Miss McLean as an able, earnest, and consecrated pastor, left First Baptist Church to go to the First Baptist Church of Augusta, Georgia. The church in Charlotte, now with a large and loyal membership, looked forward with eagerness to its mission in the city. The prayer of 54 years before had been answered. The prayer had been written in the church records of November, 1863: "May the great Head of the Church continue to bless the church and add to her till her numbers shall be greatly multiplied."

Chapter 6 | # A Growing Church in a Growing City, 1918–1943

Dr. Luther Little of Jackson, Tennessee, was given a unanimous call by the First Baptist Church of Charlotte to begin work on January 15, 1918. The invitation was made upon the recommendation of a committee composed of W. C. Dowd, J. A. Durham, T. S. Franklin, J. P. Hackney, H. G. Harper, and V. J. Guthery. Dr. Little accepted the call, and his ministry was to last for 25 years and seven months through a period of two major wars and a severe depression. It was also to be a period of unprecedented growth for the city of Charlotte as well as for the First Baptist Church.

Luther Little was born in the countryside near the beautiful little village of Tuscumbia, Alabama, the youngest of the ten children of Rufus Lafayette and Martha Ann McGaughy Little. When he was about three years old, his parents moved across the state line to Booneville, Mississippi, where he grew up and attended the public schools. At the age of twelve he was converted in the little church of the town and was baptized there. He was licensed to preach at the age of sixteen years, and immediately he began holding services in little churches and school-houses of the county.

He worked his way through Mississippi College by cleaning the chapel and washing dishes in one of the dining rooms, at the same time making a fine scholastic record and winning nearly every medal offered for debate and oratory. After graduation, he went back to his hometown, where he was ordained to the ministry. While attending the Southern Baptist Theological Seminary in Louisville, Kentucky, he preached nearly every Sunday as supply or student pastor. His first pastorate was at Brownsville, Tennessee, where he married Miss Effie Ayres of Holly Springs, Mississippi. He served as pastor of the First Baptist Church, Fort Worth, Texas,

84

for six years, during which time the couple's daughter Lucille was born.

In 1904, Dr. Little went to the First Baptist Church in Galveston, Texas, where he did an important work during the rebuilding and reconstruction after the great storm of 1900. While pastor there he held many revivals throughout Texas, and he later became an evangelist, working under the Home Mission Board and preaching throughout the South. He was called to the Tabernacle Church in Seattle, Washington, and then to the First Baptist Church in Jackson, Tennessee, where he worked among old friends. The honorary degree, Doctor of Divinity, was conferred upon him. Dr. Little was described as a great orator and a clear thinker, having an attractive pulpit personality. He was a fundamentalist in his belief in the Bible and its doctrines. During his pastorate, the First Church of Charlotte had the largest Sunday School membership and the largest church membership in the state.

Dr. Little instituted the radio broadcasting of the regular Sunday services of First Baptist Church in October, 1921, over W.B.T., later transferring to W.S.O.C. The first man in the country to broadcast a regular church service, he continued to broadcast these services throughout his ministry in Charlotte and maintained for 25 years the longest continuous and sustained radio preaching from one place in the United States. To thousands who could not attend church services, his messages brought joy and comfort.

The radio ministry was never a financial responsibility of the church. On the first Sunday of March each year, the broadcasts were set aside to receive contributions from the Radio Club who were not only members of the church, but friends and others from the radio audience. J. Russell Smith, who for many years has been one of the treasurers of the church, recalls the Sunday evening each spring when Dr. Little read over the radio the name of any person who sent in as much as a dollar. The favorite hymns of the donors were sung by the choir and the congregation. On one such occasion Wade H. Harris, the editor of *The Charlotte Observer*, wrote to Dr. Little, ". . . . The song service in the First Baptist Church is inspiring. Why can not the choir and congregation to-night sing 'Tell Me the Old, Old Story, of Jesus and His Love?' "

During the early twenties the First Baptist Church was a flowering downtown landmark. From the beginning of his ministry in Charlotte, Dr. Little took upon himself the responsibility of seeing to the comfort of the worshippers. Many years later he wrote of the early days. "Perhaps some of you do not know that through all these years I have been at the church every Sunday morning by eight o'clock looking over all the rooms and seeing that they were warm and ready and clean for your comfort. Many times when you were still asleep it has been my pleasure to be preparing for your comfort when you arrived at the building."

At First Baptist many found the answer to both their spiritual and social needs. The following excerpts from the church bulletins for 1919 and 1920 are an interesting commentary on the church life of that period.

"February 29, 1919. Silence. Silence. Silence. With the first note of the organ, divine service begins. Let all talking and confusion of any kind cease. Nothing disturbs the worshiper more than careless and unnecessary whispering; so please remember the pleasure and welfare of others."

"March 14, 1920. The Sunday School banquet given Monday evening by Mr. T. S. Franklin was one of the most enjoyable and helpful occasions of the new year. All who were present agreed." T. S. Franklin was the mayor of Charlotte from 1907 to 1909, and the superintendent of the First Baptist Sunday School for 35 years.

"May 16, 1920. On next Sunday, May 23d, our Evangelistic Campaign will begin. We are pleased to know that Dr. Little has consented to preach for us during this meeting, and we are confident that God will give us a great ingathering of souls." Eighty-six new members were added to the church during this meeting.

"July 11, 1920. On Monday evening at 8 o'clock the First Baptist Brotherhood will have a Garden Party on the lawn directly back of the Carnegie Library. There will be plenty of entertainment, refreshments and everything necessary to insure a pleasant evening."

"August 8, 1920. You should not miss the opportunity to visit the Baptist Orphanage at Thomasville next Wednesday morning, August 11, leaving here at 8:30 a.m., on the excursion which is to be under the direction of Pritchard Memorial Church. Round trip fare for adults will be $1.20, and for children, 60 cents. This is well within the reach of everyone, and it is hoped that First Baptist Church will have a large representation. Each visitor will be expected to take something good to eat; picnic dinner will be served on the Orphanage grounds. During the day the children of the institution will give an entertainment which we are sure will be very enjoyable."

"August 22, 1920. It is a distinct pleasure to have with us today as our speaker, Rev. J. B. Hipps, who has labored so faithfully for a number of years as a missionary in Shanghai, China, having been sent out by this church. He is remembered by many of our members who were delighted with the announcement that he would be with us."

"November 14, 1920. The new West Oak Baptist Chapel will be dedicated this afternoon at 3:30, and we hope that many members of this church will be present. Take the Seversville car and get off at Severs' store."

"November 21, 1920. Company H of the Ladies' Aid Society, which is to be composed of young women of the church who cannot meet in the daytime, will meet Monday evening at 8 o'clock with Mrs. Luther Little, 506 North Tryon Street. All of the young women of the church are invited whether they wish to join or not, as the meeting is to be a social as well as for business."

"December 5, 1920. As the Calendar goes to press the big beautiful Pageant is about to be presented in the City Auditorium. Further mention of the same will be made next week." The City Auditorium was on the corner of College and Fifth Streets.

"December 12, 1920. Last Tuesday evening the Philathea, 3-B Philathea, and 3-B Baraca Classes held their respective monthly business meetings at the church, followed by a joint social hour. Would this not be a good plan in the future embracing all of the organized classes?"

"December 19, 1920. A considerably large contribution of clothing and money has been received for the starving children of Europe, but it is hoped that more will feel the need of their supporting this movement and that much more will be received before Tuesday, on which day the box will be closed. Any contributions may be left in the church office."

"December 26, 1920. For the sufferers of the Near East and China we have received to the present time $783.56, which amount has been forwarded to our Foreign Mission Board, along with a box of good warm clothing valued at $600. Another remittance will be made the first of this week."

"December 26, 1920. We are glad to say that the Orphanage box this year was one of the best ever sent from our church. There was an abundant contribution of useful articles, as well as a considerable amount of money. In the name of the orphans we thank the Ladies' Aid Society of the church."

At this time First Church helped with the organization of three more Baptist churches in Charlotte. The first of these, Durham Memorial, grew from a mission Sunday school which was started on Montgomery Avenue in Seversville on June 1, 1919. About one year later First Baptist purchased a lot and erected a building which was dedicated as West Oaks Baptist Chapel. At the dedication on November 14, 1920, Dr. Little preached on "The Banquet of Love." Luther Little, L. R. Pruette, J. A. Durham, L. C. Withers, and V. J. Guthery formed the council which organized the mission into West Oaks Baptist Church on April 3, 1921. Twenty-six of the charter members were from First Baptist. The next year the property was deeded by First Church to West Oaks, and a year later the name was changed to Durham Memorial Baptist Church in honor of J. W. Durham, deacon of First Baptist Church and head of the Durham and Murphy Land Company, who had had a large part in the construction of the building.

St. John's Baptist Church was organized by a group of Baptists, many of them members of First Baptist Church, who resided in the Elizabeth section of the city. A lot was purchased on Hawthorne Lane and letters were granted to 186 members of First Baptist Church, who with others organized the church and built the building on the corner of Hawthorne Lane and Fifth Street.

Southside Baptist Church was organized as the result of weekly prayer meetings in the homes of people in the vicinity of South Boulevard and McDonald Street in 1921. Rev. T. B. Phillips started these prayer meetings and led the group in organizing the church in 1922. The council consisted of Dr. Luther Little, Dr. L. R. Pruette, Rev. J. M. Snyder, and Rev. T. B. Phillips. H. F. Darsey, a deacon of First Baptist, took an active part in starting the Sunday School and in raising the money to finance the building. Rev. Phillips was called as the first pastor.

The church realized a need for an expansion of the educational facilities and, therefore, purchased a strip of land 28' by 80' immediately to the rear of the Sunday school building. The Presbyterian Standard Publishing Company sold the land on October 19, 1919, for $2,473.52. Architect J. M. McMichael drew the plans for the $125,000 building. The parsonage at 506 North Tryon Street was sold for $20,000, which was added to the building fund. Special pledges amounted to over $80,000.

The cornerstone was laid on June 10, 1923, and in it were placed: a Bible, coin, *The Charlotte Observer*, *The Charlotte News*, a church calendar, a Sunday school quarterly, group pictures of the beginners, primaries, and juniors, photographs of Dr. Luther Little, T. S. Franklin, Earl Rason, Mrs. Alex Stephens, Mrs. A. C. Craven (church secretary), and Robert Farrar (janitor), and a copy of the church history written by Miss Carrie McLean. The building was occupied on February 24, 1924, by the Sunday school with an attendance of 1,225.

In September of the same year, an intensive enlargement campaign and revival conducted by Louis and James Entzminger was an important event. A religious census of the city was taken, methods classes and conferences were conducted, a visitation program was set up, and 35 new workers were added to the Sunday School staff. A new era of Sunday school work had begun.

The Sunday school has had many fine superintendents. A partial list includes William Boyd, W. F. Cook, C. C. Lee, R. D. Graham, Dr. O. F. Gregory, Capt. T. L. Vail, Thomas M. Pittman, J. O. Bell, W. F. Dowd, I. W. Durham, W. C. Dowd, V. J. Guthery, and T. S. Franklin. Others have been J. H. Bostic, G. D. Kilgore, S. D. Bagwell, and C. C. Martin. Since 1940 the educational director has served as superintendent.

Typical of the growth of the First Baptist Church during the 1920's was the month of January, 1925, when, on the first Sunday of the year, both morning and evening church services were held with the auditorium and gallery filled with worshippers. On that day there were 46 new members in Sunday School and 22 new church members. During the month the Business Women's League was organized with 200 members present. Mrs. P. F. Dawson was elected counselor of the group, and Miss Evelyn Rucker was selected as president. The County Sunday School Convention met in January at the young St. John's Baptist Church. In June of 1925 the first Vacation Bible School was organized with Mrs. C. A. Duckworth as director, with a chapel service each morning featuring busy men and women from the church membership who left their places of work briefly to speak to the children.

The Junior Church was organized in 1927, the first session being held on Easter morning, April 17, with 200 boys and girls meeting in the auditorium of the education building for a service adapted to their ages which ranged from six to thirteen. The director was C. A. Duckworth, and the patron deacons were C. O. Kuester and

E. W. Haight. Mr. Duckworth led the Junior Church for 27 years, using vivid visual props to teach the lessons of the Christian faith to children. Visitors frequently came from other churches to observe the methods of the Junior Church. In the youthful congregation were Carl McCraw and Clarence Kuester, Jr. They, with others, remember on their birthdays coming through a golden gate, provided by member Paul Efird of the Efird's Department Store, as their peers sang the birthday song. Mae Duckworth Hope recalls sitting in the top of a lighthouse, also given by Mr. Efird, and enthusiastically singing "Throw Out the Life-Line."

Dr. Little was a popular preacher and public speaker, responding to calls in the city ungrudgingly. On May 25, 1927, the Senior Class of Central High School came to First Baptist for their graduation sermon on "The Worthwhile Life" by Dr. Little, this being the third time he was so honored. The class wrote to the church, "We are sure every member of the Class of '27 will carry away with him the memory of the sermon as one of the finest things he experienced during the years of High School."

As the church grew, its horizons were continually widened by the inspiring preachers who were brought to the First Baptist pulpit. Dr. Little maintained a cordial relationship with many northern Baptist churches, as evidenced by the announcement in the church bulletin that he and Mrs. Little were to spend two days in Washington, D. C., attending the American Baptist Convention. A Southern Baptist Convention minister, Dr. Len G. Broughton of Atlanta, Georgia, nationally and internationally known and recognized as an eminent preacher of the gospel, held a revival meeting in October and November of 1930. As a result of this meeting, there were 225 new members added to the church including some who after 50 years are still faithful members: M. G. Perry, W. C. Leary, Marcella Berry, Ollie G. Webb, Mrs. J. H. Kline, Mrs. R. F. Thorne, Sr., James Nelson, Exum Waldrop, and John L. Ward. On their admission as members, the church prayed, "Father, make the door of this church, Thy House, wide enough to receive all who need human love, fellowship and the Father's care; and narrow enough to shut out envy, pride and hate. Make its threshold smooth that it be no stumbling block to childhood, weakness or straying feet, but rugged and strong enough to turn back the temptor's power. Father, make the door of this house the gateway to Thy eternal kingdom."

First Baptist experienced another fruitful revival in those days of the deep Depression when Dr. George W. Truett, the beloved Baptist preacher from Dallas, Texas, held a revival in March of 1931 in the Armory, sponsored by all the Baptist churches of Charlotte. Mr. M. G. Perry recalls the meeting as the most gripping and spiritual he ever attended. He remembers the compassionate countenance of Dr. Truett and his magnetism.

Throughout its history, members of First Baptist have been recognized by the community for their accomplishments both in and outside the church. Miss Carrie McLean was an attorney in the city and in 1916 the author of the first history of the church. When elected to the North Carolina Legislature in 1927, she was among the first women to serve in Raleigh. For many years she taught an adult Sunday School class at First Baptist. Clarence Kuester, Sr., a leader of the church, was the chief executive of the Charlotte Chamber of Commerce from 1921 until 1948. It was Mr. Kuester who often invited Dr. Little to the platform to offer prayer during the visits of dignitaries. In 1936 during the visit of president Franklin Roosevelt to the newly constructed Memorial Stadium, Dr. Little prayed, "We are grateful to God for our citizens in all walks of life. . . . Especially are we grateful for our human friend and President . . . Keep his body, mind, and soul safe — sheltered in Thy love. For the entire nation we pray . . ."

The year 1936 neared the peak of Dr. Little's ministry. He wrote at Christmas time, "My good wishes for the First Baptist church and her people is a part of my life. Counting the church membership, the Bible school, and other friends in the congregation, I walk with and minister to more than five thousand people . . . The happiness which I find in your fellowship knows no bounds. . . . May you find the Christ as a babe in Bethlehem and as a Savior on the cross. With every good wish that a pastor ever had for his people, I greet you this Christmas time."

By 1937 First Baptist was truly a growing church in a growing city. Charlotte, whose population was over 82,000, at this time had four skyscrapers and 1200 retail stores. It was a hub of textile manufacturing and a commercial and distribution center. The church had a membership of 3,600 and an annual budget of almost $39,000. Marshall E. Lake was chairman of the Board of Deacons. The 3-B Baraca Class consisted of 400 men and had a class budget of $1,489. The class was taught by an attorney of the city, Guy T. Carswell, and by Judge W. Vance Howard. The pastor's wife, Mrs. Luther Little, taught the First Philathea Class, and Mrs. P. F. Dawson was teacher of the 3-B Philathea Class. Mrs. Ernest S. Rothrock was president of the Business and Professional Women's Auxiliary, and Mrs. Paul Efird served as president of the Women's Missionary Union.

Employed by the church were Miss Louise Murphy, who had been the first financial secretary of the church since 1913, and Miss Ree Sheets, niece of Dr. Little, who had served as church secretary since 1927. Mr. Edward E. Rutledge, a competent musician and excellent soloist, came to First Baptist in 1935 from the Bell Avenue Baptist Church in Knoxville, Tennessee, to act as choir director and Dr. Little's assistant. His wife, Eva Rutledge, was church organist. Also employed by the church were Ida Gaddy, who served as janitress from 1925 until 1937, and Robert Farrar, who worked as janitor from 1908 until 1937. Some still remember these two faithful servants as truly blessed "door-keepers in the house of the Lord."

Concerning the down-town church, Dr. Little wrote in the *3-B Baraca Booster,* "The down-town church is always located in the midst of the city's most wicked spots as well as the city's high-class business. It must always be kept in mind that this kind of church is called upon for more things than any other church. This kind of church occupies the first-line trench in the battle of religion."

It was indeed the era of the down-town church, and many factors had contributed to the growth of First Baptist. Streetcars and then buses ran regularly to every neighborhood in the city. Downtown was the primary shopping area, the finest restaurants were there, and the public library was next door to the church. Dr. Little was a social, outgoing, friendly man, in the right place at the right time. He visited the members of the church and the citizens of the town, greeting personally every newcomer to the city. Miss Sheets, who remembers her uncle well, says, "He built the membership of First Baptist Church almost single-handed." During his pastorate the congregation grew from 1200 to 3701, and the Sunday School increased from 700 pupils to 2800.

The church under the leadership of Dr. Little worked to meet the needs of specific groups, starting programs that are commonplace today but new at that time. A class of Silent Friends met every Sunday afternoon at three o'clock. There was a Story Hour for children under nine years of age on Sundays at 6:45 P.M. Student Night was observed each year on a Sunday night during the students' Christmas holidays. When World War II erupted in December of 1941, the church was already entertaining soldiers from Camp Sutton in Monroe, North Carolina, and from Morris Field in Charlotte after services on Sundays. Soon a social hour each Sunday from five until six o'clock was inaugurated with a strong welcome to all service men and women. This hour featured fellowship, refreshments, and entertainment.

As growing numbers of their own members were called into the armed services, the church took to its heart those who from all parts of the country were stationed nearby. A radio listener wrote to Dr. Little in April of 1942, "Your prayers for our dear boys in uniform and the cause for which they are fighting hard are grand. I told several mothers yesterday to be listening next Sunday." In April of 1943 while the pastor was away at a revival meeting in Winston-Salem, the church had the good fortune of hearing Chief Chaplain Loyd W. Teague of Camp Sutton preach at Sunday worship and also two world-famed musicians who were stationed at Camp Sutton. They were Pvt. Zelik Kaufman and his accompanist, Pvt. Paul Gruber. That evening Hans Charles Newelt, a member of First Baptist who was formerly of Vienna, Austria, and who was driven from his home by the Nazi regime, spoke to the congregation.

Late in the year 1942 a new Baptist church was established in Charlotte. A group of Baptists, including a number of First Baptist members, living in the Myers Park section of the city decided that a Baptist church was needed in that area. A meeting was called in the chapel of Queens College on Sunday afternoon, December 6, to discuss preliminary plans. Myers Park Baptist Church was organized on January 17, 1943, with 162 members of First Baptist among the charter members.

On December 28, 1942, *The Charlotte Observer* noted the 25th anniversary of Dr. Little's pastorate with a long front page story. Then in January of 1943, Dr. Little announced that he would close his pastorate at First Baptist on the last Sunday in July.

May 23, 1943, was one of the most satisfying days of Dr. Little's ministry, for then the new education building was dedicated, with all church property free from debt. The building complex consisted of the auditorium built in 1909, the education building occupied in 1924, and a new Sunday School building called the Garland Court Annex. For the latter structure, the Presbyterian Standard Publishing Company's building on Garland Court just east of the church's education building was purchased on March 8, 1942, for $9,000. It was remodelled to provide an assembly room seating 200 people and six classrooms for the young people's department. The church became free of debt in 1943 after owing on its building for almost 25 years.

On the day of dedication, a great congregation was present. The church and Sunday School officers stood grouped about the pulpit as the dedicatory prayer was offered. Dr. Little prayed: "Father, these buildings are placed here in the midst of this city for Thy glory and for service to all who will accept the ministrations found herein. So we give to Thee and to saints and to sinners this earthly retreat. From this day forth may there come a new devotion and loyalty to the hearts and acts of Thy people who worship here. May this home-base be a shelter for all who desire rest, fellowship, and salvation." A vocal duet "The Lord Is in His Place" was sung by L. Deck Taylor and E. E. Rutledge. The service was closed by the giving of a gift of $1,100 to missions for the spread of the gospel.

Dr. Little retired the following July to a busy life as supply pastor and revival preacher. During the first 16 months of his retirement he preached 301 sermons. While at First Baptist, Dr. Little kept a meticulous record of his activities which included 3,658 sermons, 17,273 visits and calls, and 2,079 baptisms. He continued to be a faithful member of First Baptist until his death on January 22, 1953.

Few members of the church are aware that Dr. Little was the

author of a novel called *Manse Dwellers,* the story of a preacher and his family. As the writer depicted the character of the protagonist of his novel, he described himself: "While leading people to Heaven, he was a genuine friend on the street, a real partner with mankind in business and social relations."

Dr. Little is still remembered for his dignified presence in the pulpit, wearing a black swallow-tailed coat in winter and a white tailed coat in summer. He closed every service with a benedictory prayer, always ending with a Scriptural benediction as the one in Hebrews which he often quoted: "Now the God of peace, that brought again from the dead our Lord Jesus, that great shepherd of the sheep, through the blood of the everlasting covenant, make you perfect in every good work to do his will, working in you that which is well-pleasing in his sight, through Jesus Christ; to whom be glory for ever and ever. Amen."

Chapter 7 | A Fruitful Generation, 1943–1958

In November of 1943, the country was in the grip of World War II and the church had been without a pastor for four months. So it was with great joy and gladness that First Baptist Church of Charlotte in December greeted Dr. Casper C. Warren as the new minister.

The events surrounding the call which was extended to Dr. Warren are recalled by Mrs. J. Russell Smith, who was a member of the pulpit committee looking for a new pastor. She relates that on a Tuesday or Wednesday in October, 1943, Dr. Ralph Herring of Winston-Salem, who had served First Baptist as a supply preacher, was extended a call by the committee to come to Charlotte as pastor. Dr. Herring declined the call, but informed the committee that the right man for First Baptist was at that very time visiting his sister nearby and might be available to preach the following Sunday. Dr. Herring said that the man, Dr. Casper C. Warren, needed the challenge which First Baptist would offer, and the church needed the ministry which Dr. Warren would give.

The following Sunday morning Dr. Warren preached to the congregation, and unaware that he was being considered as the future pastor, reminded his audience of their failings. Among other things, Mrs. Smith recalls, he called the membership a bunch of loafers — and his listeners revelled in it. All Sunday afternoon the telephones of the members of the pulpit committee rang and the concensus was unanimous, "This is the man we want."

Following the morning worship service on Sunday, November 7, 1943, the church went into conference to hear the report and recommendation of the pulpit committee. The committee recommended that Dr. Casper C. Warren be extended a "unanimous call as pastor and minister and that we pledge him our full cooperation and assure him of our earnest desire to go forward under his leadership and the guidance of the Holy Spirit." Twelve or more members seconded the motion to accept the recommendations of the committee, and by a rising vote the congregation voted unanimously to call Dr. Warren.

Dr. Warren came in December from the Immanuel Baptist Church in Little Rock, Arkansas, with his wife, Mary Lashbrook Strickland Warren, and their children Mary Virginia, Casper Carl, Jr., and Alva Eugene. Marshall Lake wrote in the December, 1943, Baraca *Booster*, "Dr. Warren's education and wide experience, not only as pastor but as a leader in Southern Baptist activities, eminently qualify him to lead us in building a church program of greater service and devotion to God and our fellow man. He was trained in the law at Wake Forest College and successfully practiced that profession for several years. But his great interest and activity in church work as a layman at Dunn, North Carolina, made him receptive to the call of the ministry. That he accepted the call marks him as a man of decision and deep religious conviction. His experience as an officer in our Army in the First World War gives him an insight into a troubled world that could come in no other way." After Dr. Warren had been pastor for six months, Charles L. Goble wrote in the *Booster*, "Dr. Warren is the answer to our prayers, a Godly man who is sincere in his thoughts, a man who lives day by day for God and is not satisfied unless he is winning souls for Jesus Christ."

Dr. Warren was a native of Sampson County, North Carolina. At Wake Forest College he was graduated in law in 1917 and in the Arts in 1920. After serving as Second Lieutenant in World War I, he practiced law with attorneys Clifford and Townsend in Dunn from 1920 to 1922. Upon his surrender to the call to the ministry, he entered Southern Baptist Theological Seminary, Louisville, Kentucky, in the fall of 1922, where he earned the Th. M. and Th. D. degrees. While doing his graduate work, he served as Fellow in New Testament Interpretation under Dr. A. T. Robertson. Ouachita College conferred upon him the Doctor of Divinity dedegree in 1944, and Wake Forest College honored him with the same degree in 1948.

His first pastorate was with the Lexington Avenue Baptist Church in Danville, Kentucky, where he served for ten years, seeing an increase in membership from 120 to 1,600. In Danville Dr. Warren began the local mission program which characterized his ministry wherever he served. He went to Little Rock in 1938 and there started 11 mission stations. When he resigned to come to Charlotte, the Immanuel Church praised him as "An outstanding executive, a constant builder, a tireless worker, a missionary in its fullest meaning, and above all a true and loyal follower of the Lord Jesus Christ at all times and under all circumstances."

During Dr. Warren's pastorate at First Baptist, all the church programs were reevaluated and unified. It was under the direction of John Marvin Crowe, the new educational director, that the Sunday school was reorganized. Mr. Crowe was graduated from William Jewell College and attended the Southern Baptist Theological Seminary in Louisville for three years. Mr. Crowe came to Charlotte with a vast knowledge and experience in Sunday school and Training Union work, having been the Sunday school and Training Union secretary in Illinois for three years and associate Sunday school Training Union secretary in Missouri for six years. He served as educational director for Long Run Baptist Association in Kentucky one year and later in a similar position with First Baptist Church in Abilene, Texas. He came to First Baptist in May, 1944, to begin immediately to blend the work of all the departments of the church into one unified, church-centered program of Christian education. In seven years' time the Sunday school grew from eight departments with about 125 workers to 28 departments with about 300 workers. Attendance increased from 755 in 1944 to 1,587 in 1950. The school was recognized as a Standard School by the Baptist Sunday School Board in 1950. In the program implemented by Mr. Crowe, the trend was to smaller classes and more outreach.

When the Sunday School was reorganized in 1944, the Garland Court Annex housed a department for adults and was remodelled in 1948 to provide for two nursery departments also. The Extension Department of the Sunday school, later to be called the Homebound Department, was organized to minister to those unable to attend on Sundays because of their age, health, or Sunday work. Among the leaders of this work for many years were Ruby Caudle,

Ida Sikes, and Buford Cromer. Mrs. Minta Agnew served as co-ordinator for many years.

Along with the changes in the church program were also changes of personnel. Miss Ree Sheets, who had been the church secretary for 17 years, resigned on April 1, 1944, to accept a position with the Southern Railway. The church expressed a tribute to her efficiency in "The Church Voice": "Her usefulness and versatility have been demonstrated not only as a church secretary but as Sunday School and Training Union worker, church hostess, janitor, cook, custodian and in almost every capacity which a large and growing church demanded. She has worked neither by the clock nor for a salary but because of her genuine love for Christ and his church."

Miss Marie Roberts became educational secretary on May 1, 1944. Mr. Crowe said of her, "She has thorough knowledge of the educational program and is a tireless worker. Her records quickly reveal any information needed concerning the church program." Miss Roberts became indispensable to any member of the church who desired information or help. Two other new staff members were Mrs. W. J. Smith, Jr., who assumed the duties of financial secretary, and Mrs. Reuben K. Walker, who served as church secretary.

Mr. Edward Rutledge had resigned as minister of music in June, 1943, to accept a similar position in First Baptist Church, Newport News, Virginia. Miss Gertrude Gower became choir director in November, 1944. Mr. Robert Rodwell became the organist on September 1, 1945, coming from the Village Chapel in Pinehurst, North Carolina, where he had served for several years. Mr. Rodwell was considered among the leading organists of the state.

On behalf of the members of the church who were in military service, a Military Service Committee was formed, whose duty it was to mail "The Church Voice" regularly to those in service, to write personal letters, and to mail a gift box to each one every Christmas. A Service Honor Roll containing 579 names was displayed in the foyer of the auditorium. There was a weekly roll call of a few service men and women remembered in special prayer each Wednesday night, and a news column concerning them appeared each week in "The Church Voice."

On Christmas Eve of 1944, Dr. Warren wrote a Christmas message to his congregation: "If I had my way this Christmas I would go to your home and take a chair in your family circle for at least an hour. We'd talk of God's goodness . . . and the sufficiency of His grace. . . . I would apologize sincerely for the mistakes and failures which I have made in trying to serve as your pastor and I am sure your sympathetic understanding and forgiveness would inspire me to try to do better next year. . . . May I especially reassure each of you dear parents, wives and loved ones who have a son, husband or relative in the armed forces of our country that our hearts are with you and in so far as is possible we share in your anxiety. . . . Mindful of the unmistakable guidance of our loving Heavenly Father through the years when stupendous forces are rapidly remaking the world, let us reaffirm our faith in Him. . . . Devotedly your pastor, C. C. Warren."

As the servicemen began returning home, Marvin Crowe, educational director, and Leon Stacks, superintendent of the Young Adult Department, asked Buford Cromer to teach the Victory Class for the returnees.

First Baptist Church had a satisfying experience when Billy Graham, Charlotte's native son, held his first crusade meeting in the church in 1947. The church was soon overflowing, and the revival had to be moved to the Charlotte Armory. Bringing with him soloist George Beverly Shea and choir director Cliff Barrows, Graham wondered about the reception his hometown would give him, but the overflow audiences at the church and the Armory gave him the courage to break away from the Youth for Christ organization and form his own evangelistic team. His mother remembered sitting in the First Baptist auditorium, saying, "I remember how I broke out in a cold perspiration. You know, a lot of questions come to a mother's mind."

Dr. Warren again followed his pattern of establishing missions as part of his ministry. The first of these was Homewood, which had been organized in 1943, but in 1944 asked that First Baptist operate it as a mission. Workers from First Baptist at Homewood were O. L. Turk, R. H. Johnson, and M. G. Perry. The mission was reorganized as a church in 1952.

New Hope Mission grew from a Sunday school started by a group of people about seven miles east of Charlotte, who sought help from First Baptist. Edward C. Lovell became its superintendent and tripled its attendance within a few months. It became the New Hope Baptist Church, and during its first year divided, forming a second church, Cedar Grove.

First Baptist took over the operation of a mission on South Clarkson Street, which had had several former sponsors. Beginning with eleven people, the attendance soon grew to about 60. The workers there were O. L. Turk, M. G. Perry, and G. R. Abernathy.

The Bethel Mission was established near the Bethune Elementary School in an old residence on West Ninth Street, with Edward C. Lovell as superintendent and Don Austin as pastor. Within a year the congregation had grown to about 125, necessitating a new auditorium. Francis Stogner also served as the superintendent.

When Morris Field became a housing project after World War II was over, a barracks building was leased for church services. Several pastors worked among the transient population.

The Commonwealth Mission met for four years in the First Baptist Recreation Center on Commonwealth Avenue. The mission was self-supporting almost from the beginning and was organized into the Commonwealth Baptist Church in 1951 with 122 members.

At this time Park Road Baptist Church was organized by members of First Baptist Church, Pritchard Memorial, and St. John's Baptist Church, who recognized the need for a Baptist church in the community. After a year of planning, the church was organized in the auditorium of the Park Road Elementary School on December 10, 1950.

A great work of Marvin Crowe at First Baptist was leading in the planning of a four-story education building facing Seventh Street. The work was to be completed by Keener Pharr, who came to First Baptist as education director after the resignation of Mr. Crowe to go to Abilene, Texas, in January of 1951. Keener Pharr was a graduate of Howard College and of Southwestern Baptist Theological Seminary. He began his work in Charlotte on November 1, 1951. His previous service had been with the First Baptist Church in Birmingham, Alabama, White Settlement Baptist Church in Fort Worth, Texas, and Avondale Baptist Church in Birmingham. His educational methods were similar to those to Mr. Crowe, and his leadership was flawless.

Two attempts had been made to house the growing church membership and Sunday school attendance. In the sanctuary of the church, a beautiful marble baptistry, two side balconies, and an air-conditioning system were added in 1946. A two-story building was purchased from the Winchester Surgical and Supply Company, which was converted into educational space arranged to house two nursery departments, a beginner department, a married young people's department with four classes, and an adult department with five classes. This purchase was made in 1949, and the building was used for a while, then wrecked to make way for the new Memorial Education Building.

The new facility was to be a memorial to the fifteen young men who had made the supreme sacrifice in the service of their country during World War II, and indeed to all those who had served in the war. Those who gave their lives were W. R. Auman, Richard A. Barnes, Eugene J. Bishop, Jr., William Lester Bickett, William A. Brown, Warren M. Chapman, Robert M. DeBarry, Robert G. Graham, Jr., Eddie Lee Hall, Oscar Hunter Hammond, William D. Montgomery, Marshall Mott Shepherd, Hobart L. Sutton, Dock Graham Thomas, Jr., and Harvey D. White.

The property on Seventh Street was purchased from the J. H. Cutter Company for $48,000 in December, 1945. An adjacent plot of land was bought from the Winchester Surgical Company, the property called the Seventh Street Annex, in 1949 for $45,000. Most of 1950 was spent drawing plans, after the J. N. Pease Company, architects and engineers, were employed. A contract was let to J. L. Coe Construction Company and construction was begun in January, 1952. The beginning of the construction coincided with Dr. Warren's seventh anniversary with the church. The building was to consist of 40,000 square feet of floor space in four stories. It was to house 25 Sunday school departments, providing accommodations for 1600 persons. It would contain a suite of modern offices and a chapel, a reception area and a library.

The building was opened officially on Easter Sunday, April 5, 1953, and a memorial service and open house were held in the afternoon. The formal ceremonies, spilling onto and beyond Seventh Street, were opened by a prayer of thanksgiving offered by Keener Pharr. C. C. Martin, the chairman of the Building Committee, presented the building, and George D. Frizzell accepted it on behalf of the church. Rev. Marvin Crowe had returned from Abilene to make the dedication speech, and pastor Casper C. Warren congratulated the church on its achievement. A bronze plaque with the names of the honored servicemen was unveiled. This plaque is now in the lower lobby of the present church building. After the dedication ceremonies, there was an open house for the public in the new building.

The church bulletin for that Sunday welcomed Marvin Crowe back to First Baptist. It reads, "We count it a great pleasure to welcome back to First Baptist a former Educational Director. For seven years, 1943–1950, Marvin Crowe led this church in an educational program that brought acclaim from every section of our Convention. The foundations which he established are firm ones and in the years to come this church will continue to reap the fruits of his labors among us."

The bulletin also contained words of appreciation for Mr. C. C. Martin, the Building Committee chairman. "We are deeply in debt to Mr. C. C. Martin who has served so faithfully as chairman of the Building Committee since 1949. During these years he has devoted his time and talents to guiding our building program. No one will ever know the time he has given to this project and to him more than any other we are indebted on the occasion of the building completion. His kind and gracious spirit, his capable efficiency, his willingness to serve his Lord and church, all qualify him for the assignment he has handled so well." Serving with Mr. Martin on the Building Committee were Mrs. F. D. Burroughs, Mrs. Ben Collins, Mrs. P. F. Dawson, George D. Frizell, Paul D. Gilliam, J. C. Hendricks, J. T. Griffis, Edward C. Lovell, Jean Jeffries, Carl G. McGraw, J. C. Shepherd, W. J. Smith, Jr., Leon Stacks, Mrs. J. M. Thames, and Carl Wagner.

In 1955 Dr. C. C. Warren was honored by the Southern Baptist Convention, being elected president of that body of eight million members. He was elected on the first ballot, as the convention met in Miami, Florida. Dr. Warren was the first North Carolina pastor to be elected to that office in the convention's 110-year history. He would head the group of 29,899 churches in 30 states.

When Dr. Warren went to Kansas City, Missouri, to preside over the Southern Baptist Convention, he took with him his own minister of music, Verl Capps, to lead the singing of that great gathering. Mr. Capps was called to First Baptist from Oklahoma in January, 1953. With ability, education, and experience, he was a loyal team-player with Dr. Warren and Keener Pharr and a great blessing to the church.

During his tenure as president of the Convention, Dr. Warren challenged Southern Baptists in his president's address to establish 30,000 new preaching points by 1964. This bold challenge was voted the top news story of 1956 by the editors of Baptist papers all over the Convention. In December of 1957 Dr. Warren resigned as pastor of First Baptist to become the head of the 30,000 Movement to establish the new preaching stations. He said to the people in his church, "If I could have my way, I would never write as I must write to you now, but when I entered the ministry I promised my Lord that henceforth my way would be His way . . . I must be honest with myself and my Lord and say, firmly believing it to be His will, I must . . . undertake that which seems humanly impossible. Therefore, on this our fourteenth anniversary together, I offer my resignation as your pastor to become Director of the 30,000 Movement of the Southern Baptist Convention . . . The deepest hurt I have encountered is the thought of severing the pastoral relationship with you . . . Here we have given fourteen years of the best, the most fruitful and the happiest years of our lives . . . Good friends have advised that I should not think of accepting the position as leader of the 30,000 Movement. They say, 'It will kill you.' I can only answer in the words of Esther, 'If I perish, I perish.' "

The last Sunday in December was the pastor's last Lord's Day at First Baptist. It had been for the church, as the pastor said it had been for him, "fourteen years of the best, the most fruitful and the happiest years of our lives."

Chapter 8

The King's Business in the
Queen City, 1959–1981

The First Baptist Church of Charlotte on July 19, 1959, welcomed a new pastor, Dr. Carl E. Bates, his wife Myra and their
daughter Judy. Dr. Bates came from the First Baptist Church of
Amarillo, Texas. He was a graduate of Mississippi College and
held both the bachelor and master's degrees in theology from the
Southern Baptist Theological Seminary in Louisville, Kentucky.
Baylor University had conferred on him an honorary doctorate.

Carl Bates had declined the first call extended to him by the
Charlotte Church, offered to him at a time when the Amarillo
church was in the midst of a building program. This project was
completed during the ensuing months, and when he was given a
second call, the pastor considered his work in Texas accomplished
and was ready to come to the First Baptist Church in Charlotte.
Mrs. J. Russell Smith with other members of the pulpit committee
suspected, however, that in the era of the big hats, it was the Texas
wind that blew Myra Bates toward North Carolina. Very soon the
Charlotte congregation concurred in the reputation which Carl
Bates already had — that he was one of the finest preachers in the
Southern Baptist Convention.

Another recognized leader in Christian work joined Dr. Bates
in 1963 and remained as his co-worker for 17 years. Joe Edward
Burnette came as minister of education from Darlington, South
Carolina, where he was administrator of the Bethea Baptist Home
for the Aging. Coming with him were his wife, Ann Huguley Burnette, and their daughter Joann. Mr. Burnette received the B. A.
degree from Carson-Newman College, the M. R. E. degree from
Southwestern Theological Seminary, and also did graduate work
at the University of Tulsa, Oklahoma. He served as minister of

education at the First Baptist Church in Pasadena, Texas, and at the First Baptist Church in Baton Rouge, Louisiana. He was minister of education and associate pastor at the First Baptist Church in Columbia, South Carolina. Soon added to his duties as minister of education at the Charlotte church were those of associate pastor.

Mr. Burnette endeared himself to the members of First Baptist as a warm and sympathetic friend and counselor. During the absences of the pastor which were necessitated by his convention duties, Joe Burnette performed all the services of an able minister. In the spring of 1966, he was chosen by the Southern Baptist Foreign Mission Board to help in the Asia Sunday School Crusade in Taiwan and Hong Kong. In February of 1981 he performed a similar service in Alaska.

During the 1960's the greatest thrust of the church was its relocation to a tract of land on South Davidson and Third streets, a part of Charlotte's Urban Renewal Development. In a hotly contested decision, the church voted against moving away from the downtown area, then in a strong, cooperative movement, resolved to build again near the heart of the city.

Many members were involved in the plans of relocating the church. The Steering Committee of the Building Committee was led by C. C. Hope, Jr. Other members were Rod Alexander, Allen Bailey, Dr. Carl Bates, Gene Bobo, Joe Burnette, T. D. Clanton, Bill Cordell, Mrs. B. H. Fitzgerald, George Frizzell, Charlie Goines, G. M. Hampton, Mrs. Charles Hughston, C. C. Martin, W. E. Poe, W. J. Smith, Jr., and Mrs. H. D. Stoneham.

The Financial Campaign Committee was headed by W. E. Poe. Serving with him were Glenn Agnew, Mrs. Albert Bridges, William Cummings, Mrs. Ruth Easterling, Herman Nance, J. Russell Smith, W. J. Smith, Jr., and Leon Stacks, Sr. Chairing the Finishing and Decorating Committee was Mrs. H. D. Stoneham, serving with Mrs. F. E. Bobo, Mrs. James Estes, Forrest Eubank, Mrs. Charlie Goines, Mrs. G. M. Hampton, Mrs. David Harris, Jr., Mrs. Carl McCraw, and Mrs. J. Russell Smith.

The Construction Committee was chaired by T. D. Clanton, working with Jack Drye, Lawrence Glenn, J. T. Griffis, L. H. Rickenbacker, and J. C. Stegall. Heading the Financial Budget Committee was W. J. Smith, Jr., serving with Woodrow Brown,

Glenn Corzine, Waring Newman, W. E. Poe, Albert Warren, and Frank White, Jr. Chairman of the Furnishing Committee was George Frizzell, with Mrs. R. F. Branon, Mrs. T. D. Clanton, Mrs. Ben Collins, Harry Iden, Elizabeth Kendrick, Pauline Owen, R. G. Pittman, and Julian Underwood.

The Music Committee was composed of Mrs. Charles Hughston, chairman, with Mrs. Rod Alexander, Harvey Brown, Ray Cohn, Mrs. Kenneth England, Charles Frizen, Mrs. Clyde Harris, and William McEntire. The Grounds Committee was led by Rod Alexander, with Glenn Beckham, Edward Linsmier, R. P. Milliken, Mrs. Waring Newman, Perry Southall, and Mrs. Eugene Warren. The Insurance Committee was headed by James Estes, with Rovy Branon, Edward Lovell, and Douglas Stoneham.

The Real Estate Sale and Transition Committee was chaired by T. D. Clanton, with Harry Galloway, Max Hamilton, Carl McCraw, and Sam McMahon, Jr. The Kitchen and Fellowship Committee was led by Mrs. B. H. Fitzgerald, with Mrs. John Buckwell, F. O. Goodman, Mrs. Max Hamilton, Mrs. G. H. Johnston, Mrs. Jack Reid, and Mrs. W. J. Smith, Jr. The Recreation Committee was headed by Bill Cordell, with Mrs. Allen Bailey, Claude DeMars, Kenneth England, Edwin George, David Harris, Jr., Jack Johnson, Dr. Laird Lewis, Mrs. R. G. Pittman, and Mrs. M. O. Sutton.

The Plans Committee was chaired by F. E. Bobo, Jr., with Howard Arthur, Jr., Henry Burch, Mrs. Joe Burnette, Mrs. Glenn Corzine, Tom Crawford, Mrs. Paul Gilliam, G. M. Hampton, Mrs. C. C. Hope, Jr., M. G. Perry, Mrs. W. E. Poe, and Mrs. Allison Rogers. The Legal Committee was led by C. C. Martin, Glenn Agnew, T. J. Fletcher, Paul Gilliam, Maie Myers, and James Stephens.

The ground-breaking service on the site of the new building was held on Easter Sunday, April 11, 1971, at three o'clock in the afternoon. Pastor Carl Bates and former pastor C. C. Warren, with the Building Committee chairman C. C. Hope, Jr., broke ground. The membership was provided with small shovels to participate in the ceremony, and the speakers for the occasion were representative of the entire congregation. Words of welcome were given by F. E. Bobo, chairman of the Plans Committee. After a congregational hymn "The Church's One Foundation," the invocation was prayed by Glenn Agnew, chairman of the board of deacons. Allen Bailey, chairman of the "Extra Effort Campaign," and W. E. Poe, chairman of the Financial Campaign Committee, led the pledges to the flags. Music was presented by the church choirs, led by William Jarvis, and C. C. Hope, Jr., welcomed the special guests. Dr. C. C. Warren spoke on "The Heritage of the Past," David Abernathy, president of the Youth Councils, presented "The Promise of the Future," followed by a talk by the pastor, Dr. Carl Bates, entitled "The Challenge of the Century." The congregation sang the folk song, "Pass It On," followed by the benediction given by W. J. Smith, Jr., the chairman of the Financial Budget Committee.

The words of the pastor on that day to the people were: "Today we enter a new era in the life and work of one of America's great churches. I am profoundly grateful to God for the privilege of being with you in this significant ministry.

"It is my hope that we shall acknowledge our debt to those who have gone before us. Their faith is vindicated in us today.

"I salute you, my fellow workers in Christ, for your vision, determination, and faithfulness without which this honor would not have come.

" 'This is the day the Lord hath made. Let us rejoice and be glad in it.' "

C. C. Hope, the chairman of the Building Committee, wrote in the dedication program: "Easter Sunday 1971 is a day that will long be remembered by the members of First Baptist Church. Today marks the beginning of a long awaited dream. We have spent many months and many years seeking the path which our church should follow in its plan for the future. Decisions of tremendous import have faced us all along the way. We have carefully considered the heritage of our past, we have constantly grown in our faith in the promise of the future and we have not wavered as we marched to face the challenge of this century.

"If each of us answers that challenge with a deep spirit of personal rededication, then the groundbreaking ceremony becomes a rich symbol of the spiritual renewal of us all on this Easter Day when Christians all over the world pause to honor the Glory of Christ."

The church worshipped for the last time in the Tryon Street

building on Sunday, August 20, 1972, and moved into the new building on South Davidson Street the following Sunday. The house of worship was dedicated at the two morning services. The Guy Thomas Carswell and Clara Horn Carswell Bell Tower, given by Mrs. Carswell, was dedicated, like the church building, to the glory of God. The vows of dedication read:

"For ourselves, our children and children's children, we dedicate this house and Bell Tower. In grateful recognition of the noble leadership of former pastors and the faithful labors of former members; in affectionate remembrance of those who have gone to be with Christ; and in the name of all whose sacrificial cooperation has converted a brave dream into beautiful reality, we dedicate this house and Tower, and rededicate ourselves to God."

With the new facilities, the congregation was eager to expand its work, especially in the Sunday School. The director of youth work, Mary Glover, had come to First Baptist in October of 1966 from the First Baptist Church in Anderson, South Carolina, where she was the Director of Activities. Under her leadership, with the help of the lay workers she recruited and trained, the Junior High and Senior High divisions of the Sunday School of First Baptist, Charlotte, have become models of effective, systematic Bible study for youth. Miss Glover is often asked by the convention to hold workshops and seminars in other churches.

Other staff members of the church include Tip Cockman, minister of adult education, and Marty Gayoso and Pam Jech, the directors of children's work. Roy Gaddy for many years has served as maintenance manager of the buildings and grounds. Beloved and respected by the congregation of First Baptist Church is Edna Booker, who with her husband for many years operated the Charlotte Rescue Mission in the city, and is now the hostess of the dining room and fellowship hall of the church. These and other staff workers, along with scores of lay members, today carry on the business and mission of the church.

Dennis Bucher came to First Baptist as minister of music in April of 1975, accompanied by his musical family — wife Jackie and daughters Dana and Donna. Mr. Bucher fills many shoes well: director of church music, composer, conductor, teacher, producer of musicals, soloist, and minister to the people. His first co-worker as pianist and organist was Robert Rodwell, the excellent musician who served the church for 30 years until his retirement in 1975. Carl Bates said about Mr. Rodwell, "He has assisted magnificently in helping make the worship of God glorious." Mr. Bucher said of him, "Music immediately brought us together as friends. During the time we worked together as organist and minister of music, I gained a deep appreciation for this man." In recent years, Carol Cone, who received her education in music from Furman University, has served as organist.

After the relocation of the church, the old Byzantine structure on Tryon Street, worn but still beautiful and still dear to many hearts, stood vacant for three years. The membership rejoiced when David Reule, a member of First Baptist and a realtor, negotiated the sale of the building in the spring of 1975 to the Mecklenburg Board of County Commissioners. The acquiring of the property by the county was reminiscent of the time in 1832 when the Town Commissioners provided the use of public property for Charlotte's first Baptist revival meeting, and the time in 1855 when the church met in the courthouse to revive itself and reorganize.

The building on Tryon Street, designated as Historic Property by the Historic Properties Commission, has been developed into a cultural arts and entertainment center, a project led by the United Arts Council. The former sanctuary has become the NCNB Performance Place, retaining the beautiful stained-glass windows and the slanting floor, and seating 800 persons in the accoustically perfect theater. The 400-seat Sunday School assembly room behind the sanctuary has been converted into a rehearsal hall. The corridors have become art galleries, the library a restaurant, and the classrooms of the education building the offices of Charlotte's cultural arts organizations. Most poignant to members viewing their old house of worship is the attractive use of the old Italian marble baptistry which now frames the ticket office in the lobby.

An open, public corridor called People's Place, which connects the parts of the complex, exhibits the new and retains the character of the old. The beautifully renovated building, now called Spirit Square, remains a proud legacy for members of First Baptist Church and for the citizens of Charlotte.

During the crucial year of 1971, when the church was paying off the indebtedness on two blocks of urban renewal land and breaking ground on the 8-acre plot, the pastor, Dr. Bates, was being honored by the Southern Baptist Convention. The convention, meeting in Denver, Colorado, elected the Charlotte pastor president of the 13-million-member body. Attending the convention from First Baptist were Mr. and Mrs. Robert Pittman, Mr. and Mrs. Claude Furr, Mrs. Philip Storck, and Mrs. Grant Johnston, serving as delegates and supporting their pastor. Also present at the gathering was Joe Burnette, who was elected president of the Southern Baptist Religious Education Association.

When the convention met the following year in St. Louis, Missouri, Dr. Bates was reelected as its head. At the close of his second term, W. Perry Crouch, the General Secretary-Treasurer of the Southern Baptist Convention, assessed Carl Bates' tenure as president of the nation's largest Protestant denomination. Crouch described Dr. Bates as a peacemaker who had refused to be the instrument of separate interest groups, realizing that he had been elected to serve all Southern Baptists. In the June 11, 1972, issue of the *Biblical Recorder*, Mr. Crouch wrote that the pastor had come to the convention presidency with experience and ability held by few Southern Baptists. He had served as pastor of both rural and urban churches in several states; had been a member of the Southern Baptist Executive Committee, the Sunday School Board, and the Home Mission Board; and had served as president and vice president of the North Carolina State Convention and as president of the Texas State Convention.

As president of the Southern Baptist Convention, Dr. Bates was invited to speak in many cities. During one such visit to New Orleans, where he addressed the annual Brotherhood missions dinner at the First Baptist Church, he was presented a wall plaque by the host pastor, Dr. J. D. Gray. The plaque displayed the gold-plated key from Room 244 of the old DeSoto Hotel and was made of the wood from that door. The key was a reminder of the experience which led to Dr. Bates' career as a Baptist preacher. As a young man in 1934, just out of high school in Liberty, Mississippi, he went to New Orleans to seek his fortune. In the post-depression era, the only job he found was washing dishes at the DeSoto Hotel on Baronne Street, which provided room and board. In his room, number 244, he began to read the Gideon Bible and as a result committed his life to God. Almost forty years later when the hotel was razed, the key and door were retrieved to make the plaque which was inscribed: "Presented to Dr. Carl E. Bates, president, Southern Baptist Convention, by First Baptist Church, New Orleans, Dr. J. D. Gray, pastor. . . . From the door to the room in the DeSoto Hotel where Dr. Bates found the Lord, August 28, 1934."

In 1976, the Bicentennial year when the Southern Baptist Convention met in Norfolk, Virginia, Carl Bates delivered the final address. He cited the unity which marks Southern Baptists, enumerating the principles which bind the cooperating churches together — their historical heritage, the presence of the Holy Spirit, and the power of the Gospel. Mrs. Bates served as second vice president of the Southern Baptist Convention in 1976 and 1977, the second woman to hold the position. With great poise she presided over that large gathering. Myra Bates was an appealing public speaker. She had poise, presence, an aptitude for spontaneous and extemporaneous speaking, and — above all — had a natural gift for injecting personal and homey remarks in her speeches which warmed an audience. Her participation in any church event assured a large attendance. For 21 years she taught a Sunday School class of young women, spanning almost a generation of members.

As the church looked forward to the 1980's, a Sesquicentennial Committee was appointed to plan for the events of the celebration of the 150th anniversary of the birth of the church. The committee is composed of G. M. Hampton, chairman, Mrs. Max Craig, Frances Eppley, Mrs. Paul Gilliam, Mrs. Hal Griggs, Charles Haithcock, Mrs. C. C. Hope, Jr., Don Hughston, Pauline Owen, Marie Roberts, Rae Padgett, Mrs. Doc Thurston, Don Baucom and David Stith. These members are leading in the planning of a number of events for the celebration, including the presentation of a musical drama and an old-fashioned dinner on the grounds.

Dr. Bates, after serving the church as pastor for 21 years, resigned effective December 31, 1980, to join the faculty of the Southern Baptist Theological Seminary on February 1, 1981. Dr. Bates said, "My election to the faculty of Southern Seminary is for me a great honor as well as an unparalleled opportunity to share with a generation of preachers in a way that I never expected."

Dr. Bates' last Preacher-Graphics column in the weekly "Church Voice" was written at his request by his wife, Myra. Her farewell ended with the great benediction from the epistle to the Hebrews, which the church in 1856 had used to close the Church Covenant, and which was offered so often by Dr. Luther Little.

"Now may the God of peace, that brought again from the dead our Lord Jesus, that great Shepherd of the sheep, make you perfect in every good work to do His will, working in you that which is well pleasing in His sight through Jesus Christ; to whom be glory forever and ever. Amen."

Through the years the pastors and the people of First Baptist have encouraged the young members to surrender to the call of God to Christian vocations. Many have responded. On October 25, 1981, Joan Jennings Hope was ordained as a minister of the gospel of Christ. She was the first woman to be ordained by First Baptist Church, joining the lengthy roster of young men who have been ordained by their home church.

Today First Baptist rejoices in the blessings of its growth. It has a deaconate of 96 members and has 27 standing committees with 243 members. The Sunday School is comprised of seven adult departments, two departments for single adults, graded departments for all youth and children, and a homebound department. The church maintains a television ministry, a ministry to the deaf, a ministry to special children, a summer day camp, and a week-day school. The music department consists of two adult choirs, graded choirs for all ages, special singing groups, and handbell choirs.

After 150 years of doing the King's Business in the Queen City, the First Baptist Church of Charlotte in 1982 is again in the place where its 35 members stood in 1853. Its present members, like them, as they celebrate their 150th anniversary, are wating for the Lord to send them a leader.

Appendix

STATISTICAL CHART 1832–1980
Compiled by John Marvin Crowe and Harvey E. Brown, Sr.

Year	Baptisms	Church Members	Sunday School Enrollment	Sunday School Average Attendance	Total Gifts	Missions
1832						
1833						
1834		40				
1835						
1836	4	40				
1837						
1838	6	40				
1839						
1840	1	24				
1841						
1842		11				
1843						
1844	1	39				
1845	3	35				
1846						
1847						
1848						
1849						
1850						
1851						
1852	2	26				
1853						
1854						
1855	3	35				7.25

Year	Baptisms	Church Members	Sunday School		Total Gifts	Missions
			Enrollment	Average Attendance		
1856						
1857		53				
1858	16	74				
1859	20	97				
1860	12	110				
1861	5	117				
1862						
1863						
1864	35	143				
1865		136				
1866						
1867						
1868						
1869						
1870						
1871						
1872						
1873						
1874						
1875	29					
1876	7		180	125	1,939.35	
1877	15	161	160	111	805.03	
1878	2	163	125	90	1,135.32	
1879	3	161	150	100	1,528.28	
1880		156	143	105		
1881	27	181	159	103	1,162.50	
1882	3	178	188	115	2,775.45	
1883	6	196	224	108	8,540.17	290.29
1884	6	202	180	115	7,031.98	
1885	6	202	180	115	7,031.98	
1886	25	230	170	120	2,773.00	
1887	50	316			2,362.00	233.00
1888	5	335			2,300.00	227.00
1889	7	353			2,106.79	175.00
1890	16	371	133			
1891	16	300	197		2,064.62	290.46
1892	28	306	248		2,437.50	374.50
1893	6	329	202		5,130.19	618.19

Year	Baptisms	Church Members	Sunday School Enrollment	Sunday School Average Attendance	Total Gifts	Missions
1894	34	381	255		3,823.80	398.00
1895	13	407	279		3,374.00	379.50
1896	2	414	279		3,511.70	547.55
1897	24	414	286		2,453.50	630.46
1898	21	451	172		2,143.05	143.05
1899		476	195		3,558.17	1,558.15
1900	31	517		175	3,957.60	
1901	5	500	271	168	6,801.84	945.59
1902	6	431	299	175	5,970,66	922.64
1903	14	446	479	275	6,204.55	1,011.60
1904	9	456	579	300	4,615.56	936.31
1905	22	500	623	325	5,825.78	1,713.75
1906	28	536	737	411	7,674.67	2,482.27
1907	73	718	979	554	17,682.70	1,512.35
1908	46	814	1,056	500	20,089.57	2,496.54
1909	26	819	1,047	433	38,550.81	3,504.25
1910	56	881	1,070	430	14,379.36	2,821.47
1911	39	967	811	406	12,771.56	2,705.45

Year	Baptisms	Church Members	Sunday School Enrollment	Sunday School Average Attendance	Vacation Bible School Enrollment	Vacation Bible School Average Attendance	Training Union Enrollment	Training Union Average Attendance
1912	28	998	800	375				
1913	9	988	677	438				
1914	50	1,099	778					
1915	142	1,306	1,220					
1916	54	1,242	1,234					
1917	68	1,442	1,245					
1918	57	1,599	1,047				34	
1919	62	1,798	1,055					
1920	80	1,498	1,145					
1921	50	1,550	1,075				200	
1922	130	1,564	1,261	850			160	
1923	24	1,671	1,470				113	
1924	79							
1925	171						300	

Year	Baptisms	Church Members	Sunday School		Vacation Bible School		Training Union	
			Enroll-ment	Average Atten-dance	Enroll-ment	Average Atten-dance	Enroll-ment	Average Atten-dance
1926	102	2,666	2,280	1,075	231	165	199	
1927	79	2,879	2,295	1,075	300	225	200	
1928	103	3,065	2,000	1,000			140	
1929	38	3,180	2,038	1,050			184	
1930	88	3,412	1,922	1,134			186	
1931	162	3,671	2,359	1,108			152	
1932	71	3,717	2,149	1,151			126	
1933	69	3,719	2,177	995			75	
1934	88	3,809	2,029	984			86	
1935	69	3,857	2,540	895			91	
1936	77	3,876	2,710	977			124	
1937	96	3,600	2,726	993	42	30	163	
1938	63	3,607	2,901	1,124	160	120	158	
1939	78	3,704	3,120	984	221	165	153	
1940	33	3,674	3,028	1,012	194	150	171	
1941	63	3,733	3,130	960	180	144	252	
1942	79	3,789	2,903	941	158	126	176	
1943	113	3,637	2,605	833	150	127	178	
1944	43	3,073	2,610	755	275	207	205	
1945	100	2,956	2,536	924	265	211	308	
1946	142	3,069	2,617	1,183	302	245	374	206
1947	121	3,173	2,789	1,308	328	268	402	251
1948	180	3,339	3,031	1,257	646	524	667	338
1949	105	3,384	3,250	1,487	559	469	718	387
1950	122	3,400	3,464	1,587	739	607	709	419
1951	154	3,412	3,488	1,543	907	714	656	773
1952	105	3,328	3,265		734		609	384
1953	123	3,390	3,333	1,542	1,053	857	720	450
1954	222	3,577	3,837	1,857	1,048	842	988	557
1955	155	3,740	3,985	1,910	1,074	872	1,088	605
1956	174	3,703	4,192	1,916	1,255	1,025	1,209	658
1957	178	3,885	4,117	1,994	1,167	1,043	1,218	688
1958	112	3,830	4,013	1,929	1,254	1,051	1,195	672
1959	185	3,914	3,862	1,941	1,221		1,199	633
1960	69	3,495	3,323	1,750	756		907	562
1961	110	3,492	3,105	1,491	787		849	458
1962	52	3,465	2,966	1,486	752		684	381

Year	Baptisms	Church Members	Sunday School Enroll-ment	Sunday School Average Atten-dance	Vacation Bible School Enroll-ment	Vacation Bible School Average Atten-dance	Training Union Enroll-ment	Training Union Average Atten-dance
1963	59	3,308	2,978	1,551	654		713	394
1964	76	3,265	2,871	1,475	825		711	352
1965	59	3,297	2,966	1,485	764		622	341
1966	80	3,419	2,991	1,536	790		678	368
1967	38	2,994	2,337	1,272	450		469	237
1968	30	2,564	2,220	1,167	380		453	215
1969	41	2,561	2,170	1,192	381		428	196
1970	45	2,580	2,180	1,098	320		408	196
1971	43	2,626	2,002	994	358		352	189
1972	38	2,631	2,011	974	282		329	222
1973	33	2,640	2,023	1,044	222		274	131
1974	33	2,554	2,181	1,021	215		220	156
1975	32	2,476	1,995	1,099	35		219	130
1976	26	2,417	2,124	1,039	353		191	138
1977	34	2,393	2,012	1,019	419		138	97
1978	22	2,364	1,982	969	471		134	204
1979	24	2,347	1,817	920	473		115	200
1980	21	2,323	1,876	912	471		109	–

FINANCIAL RECORD 1952–1980

Year	W.M.U. Enroll- ment	Value of Church Property	Debt on Church Property	Total Gifts	Local Expense	Missions
1952	489	849,606	135,100	227,185	178,776	48,409
1953	506	1,500,000	370,920	613,089*	578,973*	34,116
1954	494	1,541,879	336,846	262,350	196,288	55,127
1955	498	1,566,879	341,884	303,657	241,323	61,513
1956	528	1,570,879	304,196	309,106	254,826	46,356
1957	555	1,570,879	271,912	313,245	302,485	51,017
1958	551	1,570,879	184,735	287,957	233,995	61,942
1959	526	1,624,362	223,772	356,832	363,616	61,357
1960	607	1,624,362	170,148	341,168	263,487	66,884
1961	622	1,624,362	142,099	326,513	244,729	77,026
1962	621	1,624,362	109,322	334,077	246,904	76,803
1963	644	1,812,349	102,000	331,798	166,798	99,091
1964	563	1,745,000	42,474	338,661	184,379	96,373
1965	482	1,828,460	100,103	379,560	341,701	93,952
1966	527	1,791,761	86,439	391,300	210,175	91,506
1967	508	1,825,000	—	378,707	192,442	105,430
1968	490	1,801,224	26,619	419,409	449,737	87,817
1969	476	2,158,463	45,000	425,512	330,345	95,167
1970	388	2,218,450		482,822	388,423	94,576
1971	431	2,604,000	298,000	577,895	778,034**	96,224
1972	403	3,267,862	1,624,000	699,376	1,856,000***	91,559
1973	511	3,209,000	1,643,073	670,062	414,411	112,578
1974	344	4,675,000	1,585,478	648,994	619,913	110,248
1975	373	4,674,539	1,141,938	613,232	811,670	134,765
1976	461	4,674,539	1,067,687	624,743	468,710	160,808
1977	452	3,083,397	1,005,524	681,118	462,473	15,549
1978	494	3,126,935	913,763	734,784	497,315	139,069
1979	421	3,141,015	845,586	875,815	743,142	154,613
1980	385	3,065,229	783,372	1,039,685	831,594	246,724

*New Building and Equipment (429,682)
**Includes 487,535 paid on new construction
***Includes 1,612,465 paid on new construction

DECLARATION OF FAITH

(As agreed to by the Charlotte Baptist Church of Christ, September 8, 1856)

I. We believe the Holy Bible was written by men divinely inspired, and is a perfect treasure of heavenly instruction; that it has God for its author, salvation for its end, and truth without any mixture of error for its matter; that it reveals the principles by which God will judge us; and therefore is, and shall remain to the end of the world, the true center of Christian union, and the supreme standard by which all human conduct, creeds, and opinions should be tried.

II. That there is one, and only one, true and living God, whose name is Jehovah, the Master and Supreme Ruler of heaven and earth; inexpressibly glorious in holiness; worthy of all possible honor, confidence, and love; revealed under the personal and relative distinctions of the Father, the Son, and the Holy Ghost, equal in every divine perfection, and executing distinct but harmonious offices in the great work of redemption.

III. That man was created in a state of holiness under the law of his Maker, but by voluntary transgression fell from that holy and happy state; in consequence of which all men are now sinners, not by constraint, but choice.

IV. That the salvation of sinners is wholly of grace, through the mediatorial offices of the Son of God, who took upon Him our nature, yet without sin; honored the law by His personal obedience, and made atonement for our sins by His death; being risen from the dead, He is now enthroned in heaven; and, uniting in His wonderful person the tenderest sympathies with divine perfections, is in every way qualified to be a suitable, a compassionate, and an all-sufficient Savior.

V. That the great gospel blessing which Christ of His fullness bestows on such as believe upon Him is justification; that justification consists in the pardon of sin and the promise of eternal life on principles of righteousness; that it is bestowed not in consideration of any works of righteousness which we have done, but solely through His own redemption and righteousness; that it brings us into a state of most blessed peace and favor with God, and secures every other blessing needful for time and eternity.

VI. That the blessings of salvation are made free to all by the gospel, that it is the immediate duty of all to accept them by a cordial and obedient faith, and that nothing prevents the salvation of the greatest sinner on earth except his own voluntary refusal to submit to the Lord Jesus Christ, which refusal will subject him to an aggravated condemnation.

VII. That in order to be saved, we must be regenerated, or born again; that regeneration consists in giving a holy disposition to the mind, and is effected in a manner above our comprehension, or calculation, by the power of the Holy Spirit, so as to secure our voluntary obedience to the gospel and that the proper evidence is found in the holy fruit which we bring forth to the glory of God.

VIII. That election is the gracious purpose of God, according to which He regenerates, sanctifies, and saves sinners; that being perfectly consistent with the free agency of man, it comprehends all the means in connection with the end; that it is a most glorious display of God's sovereign goodness, being infinitely wise, holy, and unchangeable; That it utterly excludes boasting, and promotes humility, prayer, praise, trust in God, and active imitation of His free mercy; that it encourages the use of means in the highest degree; that it is ascertained in all who believe the gospel; is the foundation of Christian assurance, and that to ascertain it with regard to ourselves, demands and deserves our utmost diligence.

IX. That such only are real believers who endure to the end; that their persevering attachment to Christ is the grand mark which distinguishes them from superficial professors; that a special providence watches over their welfare, and they are kept by the power of God through faith unto salvation.

X. That a visible church of Christ is a congregation of baptized believers, associated by covenant in the faith and fellowship of the gospel; observing the ordinances of Christ; governed by His laws, and exercising the gifts, rights and privileges vested in them by His word; that its only proper officers are bishops or pastors, and deacons, whose qualifications, claims, and duties are defined in the Epistles to Timothy and Titus.

XI. That Christian baptism is the immersion of a believer in water in the name of the Father, Son, and Holy Ghost, to show forth in a solemn and beautiful emblem our faith in a crucified, buried and risen Savior; that it is a prerequisite to the privileges of church relation; and to the Lord's Supper, in which the members of the church by the use of bread and wine are to commemorate together the dying love of Christ, preceded always by a solemn self-examination.

WOMAN'S MISSIONARY UNION
(Compiled by Mrs. Granville M. Hampton)

Little information is contained in the records concerning Woman's Missionary Union work. There were 20 circles in the society in 1927 when Mrs. J. A. Yarbrough was president. The W. M. U. has had a fully graded organization for many years. It has made liberal offerings to the missionary cause and has observed the special weeks of prayer.

Some of the presidents or directors have been:

Mrs. T. S. Franklin, 1916–1918
Mrs. Richard C. Springs, 1919–1920
Mrs. P. F. Dawson, 1921–1923, 1947–1948
Mrs. J. A. Gardner, 1924–1925, 1934
Mrs. J. A. Yarbrough, 1926–1927
Mrs. Guy Carswell, 1928–1929
Mrs. E. B. Gentry, 1931–1932
Mrs. H. M. Short, 1935–1936
Mrs. Paul H. Efird, 1939
Mrs. W. J. Nolan, 1940–1941
Mrs. W. H. Harvey, 1942
Mrs. Cooper E. Taylor, 1943–1944
Mrs. H. B. Herndon, 1945–1946
Mrs. H. I. Grimes, 1949–1950
Mrs. C. C. Helms, 1951–1953
Mrs. E. L. Harkey, 1953–1955
Mrs. Rovy F. Branon, 1955–1962
Mrs. G. H. Johnston, 1962–1964, 1975–1976
Mrs. T. D. Clanton, 1964–1966
Mrs. C. S. Goines, 1966–1967
Mrs. G. M. Hampton, 1967–1969
Mrs. Philip D. Storck, 1969–1971
Miss Nancy Lee Kistler, 1971–1973
Mrs. Forrest Eubank, 1973–1975
Mrs. J. E. Taylor, 1976–1978
Miss Marie Roberts, 1978–1981

The title of W. M. U. President was changed to W. M. U. Director in 1968. By 1970 the name Woman's Missionary Society had been changed to Baptist Women, Young Woman's Auxiliary had been changed to Baptist Young Women, Girls' Auxiliary to Girls in Action, and Sunbeam Band to Mission Friends.

The State W. M. U. Convention met in First Baptist Church of Charlotte in 1951 and 1954. By 1963 Ovens Auditorium had been built, and the State W. M. U. Convention was held there.

FIRST BAPTIST CHURCH STAFF
(Compiled by Agnes and Paul Gilliam)

Agnew, Mrs. R. E. — Church Visitor, 1952–1963
Bobbitt, Rev. David E. — Assistant to the Pastor, 1957
Boger, Mrs. C. S. — Director of Children's Education, 1963–1974
Booker, Mrs. Edna — Church Hostess, 1973–
Brooks, Joanna — Pastor's Secretary, 1962–1966
Brookshire, Mrs. Elizabeth — Church Hostess, 1958–1973
Broome, Janice P. — Secretary/Receptionist, 1976–
Brown, Ella — Maid
Bucher, Dennis P. — Minister of Music, 1975–
Burgin, Penta — Pastor's Secretary, 1956–1961; 1961–Nov. 1962
Burnette, Ann — Director of Day School, 1973–1975
Burnette, Rev. Joe — Minister of Education/Associate Pastor, 1963–
Capps, Verl — Minister of Music, 1953–1959
Cockman, W. T. — Director of Adult Education, 1978–
Collier, Mrs. L. E. — Church Hostess, 1956–1958
Cone, Carol B. — Organist, 1977–
Cordell, Bill — Summer Recreational Director, 1963–
Crowe, J. Marvin — Minister of Education, 1944–1951
Culp, Richard — Janitor
Davenport, Cleveland H. — Janitor, 1948–
Deese, Judy — Ass't. Secretary, 1960–1961; Educ. Sec'y, 1961–1964
Drye, Mrs. Jack — Financial Secretary, 1963–1973
Eppley, Russell — Staff Assistant, 1959–1960
Estridge, R. T. — Maintenance Superintendent, 1956–1965
Farrar, Robert — Janitor, 1908–1937
Fields, L. W., Jr. — Staff Assistant, 1958–1959
Fields, William A. — Staff Assistant, 1956–1958
Ford, Mrs. Walter — Pastor's Secretary, 1970–1971
Gaddy, Ida — Maid, 1925–1937
Gaddy, W. R., Sr. — Maintenance Superintendent, 1969–
Gayoso, Marthel — Director of Children's Education, 1977–1978; Director of Day School & Preschool, 1978–1981
Glover, Mary — Youth Director, 1966–

Gower, Gertrude — Choir Director, 1944–1949
Graham, Ruth — Youth Director, 1951–1954
Grant, Maxine —— Music Assistant, 1960–1961
Hall, Mrs. Doris — Financial Secretary, 1973–1978
Harris, James — Minister of Adult Work, 1967–1971
Heifner, Betty — Youth Director, 1957–1959
Herman, Betty — Financial Assistant, 1978–
Hilburn, Mrs. Luella — Assistant Secretary, 1961–1962
Hollifield, Mrs. Howard — Coordinator of Nursery, 1966–
Howell, Alwyn — Minister of Music, 1950–1951
Hutchins, Elizabeth — Director of Children's Education, 1953–1957
Ivey, James A., Jr. — Minister of Education, 1959–1962
Jarvis, Bill — Minister of Music, 1965–1972
Jech, Pamela — Director of Children's Education, 1978–
Kistler, Nancy — Young Adult Director, 1960; Music Secretary, 1967–1971
Lewis, Mary Ann — Pastor's Secretary, 1971–1972; Financial Secretary, 1978–
Litaker, Mrs. Melvin — Education Secretary, Pastor's Secretary, 1967–1970
Markley, Mrs. James N.— Pastor's Secretary, 1972–1973
Martin, C. C. — Business Administrator, 1965–1973
Mason, Mrs. Buford — Music Secretary, 1971–
Metcalfe, Mrs. Audrey — Director of Day School, 1975–
Michaux, Mrs. C. H. — Church Hostess, 1952–1956
Mitchell, Mrs. Sue — Financial Secretary, 1960–1963
Morgan, James Q. — Recreational Director/Youth Director, 1961–1965
Murphy, Louise — Financial Secretary, 1913–1943
Neal, Charles — Assistant to the Pastor, 1955–1956
Nolan, Rev. J. W., Jr. — Assistant Pastor, 1960–1967
Norton, Billy — Staff Assistant, 1960–1961
Norton, Mrs. W. M., Sr. — Educational Secretary, 1971–1975
Oates, Zella — Receptionist/Office Secretary, 1962–
Oetzman, Mrs. Helen — Ass't. Financial Secretary, 1962–1973
Pharr, Keener — Minister of Education, 1951–1959
Pressley, Joyce — Pastor's Secretary, 1946–1954
Price, Mrs. J. E. — Financial Secretary, 1952–1960
Price, Joe — Staff Assistant, 1951–1953
Price, Mike — Staff Assistant, 1954–1955
Rackley, Ed R. — Minister of Music, 1972–1974

Roberts, Marie — Educational Assistant, 1944–1974
Rodwell, Robert — Organist, 1952–1974
Rutledge, Edward E. — Minister of Music, 1935–1943
Rutledge, Mrs. Edward E. — Organist, 1935–1943
Sheets, Ree — Church Secretary, 1927–1943
Smith, Sara Anne — Educational Secretary, 1975–
Sloan, Wendell — Minister of Education/Business Administrator, 1973–
    1978
Stroupe, J. Carson — Maintenance Superintendent, 1965–1968
Sutter, Bill — Minister of Music, 1960–1964
Swaity, Mrs. Paul — Music Secretary, 1965–1967
Turk, Mary Katherine — Assistant Secretary, 1958–1960
Warren, Linda — Pastor's Secretary/Music Assistant, 1974–1978
Whitaker, Jeanne — Youth Director, 1956–1957
White, Charles W. — Interim Minister of Music, 1951–1952
White, Laura (Mrs. R. W.) —— Organist, 1975–1977
Worley, Lorraine — Educational Secretary, 1959–1961

Index

Window On Our Past

This photo shows the interior of the old First Baptist Church sanctuary before it was converted to Spirit Square's Performance Place.

Have a historical photo you'd like to share? Send it to Mecklenburg Neighbors, The Charlotte Observer, P.O. Box 32188, Charlotte, N.C. 28232. It will be returned.

Window On Our Past

At the turn of the century, when Charlotte's First Baptist Church was known as Tryon Street Baptist, members worshiped in this structure. It was razed to make way for the structure on North Tryon that is now the home of Spirit Square arts center. *Have a historical photo you'd like to share? Send it to Mecklenburg Neighbors, The Charlotte Observer, P.O. Box 32188, Charlotte, N.C. 28232. It will be returned.*

ecklenburg Readers
Classifieds. $2 Pays
r Ad For 2 Days.

AD Complete and mail the coupon. No orders by phone. However, call 379-6631 Monday-Friday 8:30 a.m.-3 p.m. if you have a question.

out, use white-
o headline.

etter, numeral,
You may continue
when.

unt as a full line in

our cost is the

e and add $1 to
e.

n just one line as a
type or with a
e, use no more
left of the grid
0 cents per line of

3. Payment must accompany ad. Cost is at right of the grid. The minimum is $2, for which you may use up to four lines.

4. If mailing your ad, enclose a check or money order (payable to Knight Publishing Company), and mail to the address below. Mailing cash is risky. If hand-delivering to Knight Publishing Co at 600 S. Tryon St. (8 a.m.-4:30 p.m. Monday through Friday) use cash, check or money order.

5. Your ad is published first on Sunday, and again the following Wednesday; there are no cancelations.

6. Sorry, no business, real estate or rental advertising is accepted. These ads are for individuals selling items they own.

7. Wording is subject to advertising guidelines. The right is reserved to accept, reject or revise subject matter or phraseology deemed objectionable.

8. Mecklenburg Neighbors, The Charlotte Observer and Knight Publishing Co. may not be held liable should publication be interrupted or should ads ordered be omitted.

CLIP AND MAIL

The Type Ad You Want

ce **Jumbo Head**

GET ATTENTION

am- For each line of jumbo type you